FEARON'S

Careers

Marna Owen

Globe Fearon Educational Publisher
Paramus, New Jersey

Paramount Publishing

Pacemaker Curriculum Advisor: Stephen C. Larsen

Stephen C. Larsen holds a B.S. and an M.S. in Speech Pathology from the University of Nebraska and an Ed.D. in Learning Disabilities from the University of Kansas. In the course of his career, Dr. Larsen has worked in the Teacher Corps on a Nebraska Indian Reservation, as a Fulbright senior lecturer in Portugal and Spain, and as a speech pathologist in the public schools. A full professor at the University of Texas at Austin, he has twenty years' experience as a teacher trainer on the university level. He is the author of sixty journal articles, three textbooks, and six widely used standardized tests, including the Test of Written Learning (TOWL) and the Test of Adolescent Language (TOAL).

The Author: Marna Owen

Marna Owen is a well-known West Coast writer and instructional designer who specializes in educational and training materials. She has written numerous texts and supporting materials in the areas of health, English, economics, history, and government.

Subject Area Consultant: James P. Greenan, Ph.D.

Dr. James P. Greenan is Professor and Chair of Vocational Education in the School of Education at Purdue University. His instructional and research interests and expertise are in the areas of special-needs learners and generalizable skills instructional interventions. He has taught at the secondary and postsecondary levels and has served on the editorial boards of several vocational and special-needs journals.

About the Cover Photograph: © *The Stock Market/Gabe Palmer,* 1991. Environmental workers are needed more than ever today as the planet's natural resources face ever-increasing danger. Here, environmental workers test polluted water. For more information about environmental careers, see Chapter 15.

Supervising Editor: Stephen Feinstein
Editor: Joseph T. Curran
Production Editor: Teresa R. Thomas
Text Design: Dianne Platner
Composition: The Cowans
Cover Design: Mark Ong, Side by Side Studios
Photo Acknowledgments: See page *xi*.

ISBN 0–8224–0846–5

Printed in the United States of America

3. 10 9 8 7 6
Cover Printer/NEBC

DO

Contents

Unit Three: Exploring Careers

Unit Four: More Careers to Consider

Unit Five: Preparing for a Career

Unit Seven: Success on the Job

Unit Eight: Lifelong Learning

Appendix

Photo Acknowledgments

A Note to the Student

Have you ever worked on a project and found that when you were finished you had more energy than when you started? If so, you experienced something wonderful. You were doing work that was meaningful, rewarding, and fun.

Most of us would like to have this experience every day of our lives. We'd like to get up in the morning and look forward to what lies ahead. We'd like to spend our days doing work we enjoy. We'd also like to go to sleep at night knowing we did our best. We'd like a whole lifetime of work that is meaningful, rewarding, and fun. We would like a great career.

Does having a great career mean being rich, famous, and powerful? Does it mean changing the world? It can. But more often it means simply doing something we like and doing it well. Beth, who loves watching soap operas, writes for an entertainment magazine. She's paid to watch daytime TV and write about what she sees. Tom loves doing physical things. He makes a living removing large trees. Jean has a strong interest in machines and new technology. She helps install new phone systems in small businesses. None of these people are rich, famous, or powerful. But they all think they have great careers because they're doing things they enjoy.

This book is for people who want to create their own great careers—careers that are just right for them. *Fearon's Careers* will introduce you to a career-planning process. As you work through this process, you'll discover important things about the world and about yourself. You will also learn and practice skills to prepare you for finding work that is right for you. Once you learn these skills, you will be able to practice them again and again throughout your life as you and the world change.

To get the most out of *Fearon's Careers*, it is a good idea to apply what you learn. For example, you will read about several things that you can do to explore different career areas. It is not enough to just know about these techniques. You must go out and use them if they are to be of real value to you. The same goes for all of the ideas, resources, and skills covered in this book.

Planning a Career

Chapter 1
Why Plan a Career?

Many successful people hire other people to manage their careers. Most of us are our own career managers.

Chapter Learning Objectives

- Explain what a career is.
- List three rewards of working and of having a career.
- Describe the seven steps used to plan a career.
- List three things you save by planning your work life.

Words to Know

application   a form that a worker fills out when applying for a job

career   a chosen occupation

career ladder   a series of jobs that lead to greater responsibility and usually more money

competition   an attempt to get something that others want; a contest

flexible   easily changed; bending easily

income   the money a person receives, usually for working or for providing a service

pension   a regular payment to a retired person by a former employer

production   the act of making something

promotion   a change to a higher position or level

resource   something that is available that we need or can use

security   a feeling of safety; freedom from danger

technology   the use of science to create new or better products or methods of production

values   the principles that a person holds to be important; standards or beliefs

---

It is a sunny afternoon in the countryside of Italy. The year is 1400. Sixteen-year-old Antonio works beside his father in the vineyards. Sweat soaks their shirts as they pick the grapes that will be made into wine.

The father stops and stretches, his back aching with the hard work.

"Antonio. This work is for the young. Soon I will turn the farm over to you."

Antonio takes a deep breath. It is time to tell his father what is in his heart. "Father, I do not want to be a farmer. I find the work boring. Music is my love. I'm sure that if I went to the city I could become a court musician for the prince."

The father scowls. "Nonsense. It is tradition for a son to take the profession of his father. You will be a farmer, like it or not."

Antonio raises his voice. "Let my sister Maria become the farmer. She's better at growing things than I am."

"Now you are talking like a madman," Antonio's father says. "Maria will marry the man I choose and raise a family, as all girls must. Get back to work before I have the doctor bring leeches to suck the craziness from your blood!"

Antonio is angry as he yanks the fruit from the vines. He wonders when young people will be able to do what they love—instead of what they're told.

Your Career Is Your Choice— and Your Responsibility

Suppose you could bring Antonio and Maria to the United States in the 1990s. What might they be surprised to learn about working in this time and place?

You could tell Antonio that a young man is no longer expected to make a living the same way his father does. The son of a farmer may indeed become a farmer if he wishes. However, he may also seek employment as a mechanic, a writer, or even a rock star. You could tell Maria that these days more and more women have jobs outside the house. The number of women doctors, lawyers, and government leaders is growing each year. Maria would probably be happy to hear that she could marry a man of her *own* choosing rather than her father's.

Like everyone in the United States, Maria and Antonio would be free to choose their careers. However, with freedom comes responsibility. No one in the United States is *guaranteed* work. The U.S. job market is based upon **competition**. People who want to be hired often have to show that they'd be the best workers. Employers sometimes receive hundreds of **applications** for a single job.

In 1900, about 18 percent of the work force in the United States were women. By 1991, the figure had risen to 45 percent. What do you think the percentage will be in the year 2000?

Still, there are many opportunities in the United States. Some 15 million organizations hire people to do work that ranges from clearing tables to managing offices to running large companies. Schools and job training programs help career seekers develop their skills and talents. Career counselors, government agencies, and many other career **resources** are available.

This book is a resource. It is about choosing a career that is right for you. It will help you identify and use the resources around you to get you started in your career. It will give you tips to help you grow throughout your career. Reading this book is a good first step in becoming your own career manager.

Careers Practice

Answer these questions on a separate sheet of paper.

1. In terms of your career, what important freedom do you have?

2. How might competition affect your career?

3. Name three resources to help you succeed in finding a career.

What Exactly Is a Career?

Dictionaries define a **career** as "a chosen occupation" or "one's chosen life work." That is a good short explanation of the word, but there's a little more to it.

- *A career is something you choose.*

As a child, someone might have asked you what you wanted to be when you grew up. You may have answered police officer, fire fighter, teacher, or some other occupation that seemed exciting or that you

The original meaning of the word "career" was race course. Why might career seekers today feel as though they are on a race course?

admired. Now that you are older, you should again ask yourself, "What interests me? What would I like to do?" The plans you make and carry out in terms of your career are your choice—not something you're forced to do or that you just stumble into.

- *A career brings some rewards.*

People choose their careers because they offer certain meaningful rewards. Quite often, the reward is money. Most adults work because money is needed to buy food, clothing, and shelter.

However, people often choose their careers for other rewards as well. A woman who starts a small business may love being the boss and making her own hours. A social worker who helps the homeless find shelter is rewarded because he believes he's making the world a better place. An artist may be rewarded by the beauty of what she has painted or drawn. A stay-at-home father may be rewarded by watching his child grow.

These careers often have low to average **incomes**. In the case of being a parent, there's no income at all. Yet these careers are chosen by people because they fit their **values** and lifestyles. They give people what they want at a particular time.

Work itself is very valuable to us. It helps us discover who we are. It gives us a chance to learn how to use our time and energy wisely. By working we connect with the people around us and contribute to the world. Work can offer us a sense of satisfaction and accomplishment.

- *A career is a long-term but not necessarily a lifetime activity.*

People in your grandparents' generation may have told you how they chose a career early in life and then stuck to it through thick and thin. They may have worked their way up in a company and stayed loyal until retirement. For many, the biggest reward was job

What kinds of rewards might this instructor be getting from his career?

security. They felt they would always have a steady paycheck and a **pension** when they retired.

In the 1990s, workers have to be more **flexible**. A TV news reporter might hop from station to station to find the best salary and working conditions. A computer programmer may switch careers in mid-life to start his own restaurant. A homemaker may become a car salesperson when her children leave home.

As you will see in Chapter 2, **technology** quite often changes the nature of our jobs. For example, computerized robots in some factories now do much of the work that people once did. Frequently, companies move from state to state to lower their labor and **production** costs. People often have to move to where the jobs are.

For these reasons, a "long-term" career in the 1990s might last for only five years. Today's career security comes from being flexible.

- *A career gives you a chance to develop your talents.*

Martha Smith has been a nursing home aid for 30 years. She takes care of elderly people who can't live by themselves. Martha has kept up with the latest medical advances. She treats her patients well. She is always coming up with new activities for them. Martha has had a few modest pay raises, but she'll never be rich. On the other hand, Martha is the most respected aid in the nursing home. She's the one who trains all the new aids.

Martha's daughter Louise is the manager of a discount clothing store in a nationwide chain. Louise worked her way up from sales clerk to store manager. She is now trying to get a **promotion** to manage several stores. In five years, she plans to be an executive at the national level. Unlike Martha, Louise is working her way up a **career ladder**. As she does so, she is getting more responsibilities and larger pay checks.

Which of these women has a career? They both do, and they are both successful. A career does not necessarily mean you are always being promoted or getting more money. It *does* mean having a position in which you strive to do your best.

Careers Practice

Answer these questions on a separate sheet of paper.

1. What are some of the rewards you can get from a career or from work in general?

2. Give one reason why workers in the 1990s must be flexible.

3. What is meant by a *career ladder*?

How to Plan a Career

A career can be very rewarding. Finding the right career can be a challenge. How do you go about it?

This book will take you through some key steps in planning a career. Here is a quick look at what this book covers:

Parenting and volunteering are unpaid careers that promise rewards other than money.

- *Step 1. Take a look at the big picture.*

What are the fastest-growing jobs in the United States? Which jobs promise the most opportunity? What kind of education and training will workers need by the year 2000? Unit One of this book tries to answer these questions.

- *Step 2. Assess yourself and your lifestyle choices.*

What are your values, interests, and skills? What rewards do you want from a career? What resources can help you choose and succeed in your career? Unit Two will help you find out.

- *Step 3. Explore different careers.*

Many times, people accept jobs without really knowing what it would be like to work at them day after day. Once they begin working, they are surprised and sometimes disappointed. Units Three and Four of this book will give you some techniques for exploring careers. They will also provide key information on popular and growing career areas. With this information, you can be realistic about what to expect from different careers.

- *Step 4. Build a foundation for your career.*

What do you do after you have decided to pursue a particular career? In Unit Five, you will learn how to make a career plan. Part of that plan is deciding how to get the education, skills, and experience you will need. The chapters in this unit will also help you see how to follow through with your plan.

- *Step 5. Get hired.*

Starting a career doesn't always mean getting a paid job. Some people choose to be stay-at-home parents, for example. Others have careers in volunteer agencies. But most of us, at some time in our lives, will have to compete for a job or even an unpaid position as part of our careers. Unit Six will take you through the nuts and bolts of getting a job. It includes information on how and where to apply, and how to do well in an interview.

- *Step 6. Be successful.*

Many things can affect your quest for success, including your attitudes about the people you work with. Unit Seven will look at this area and show you how to avoid problems.

- *Step 7. Continue planning.*

Career planning is a lifelong process. The average U.S. citizen will change jobs seven times. Many people will switch job fields entirely at least once in their lives. It is up to you to keep being an active manager of your career. That is what Unit Eight is about.

The Benefits of Planning a Career

Does managing your career sound like a lot of work? Well, in some ways it's a job in itself. It takes time, energy, and careful planning. So why do it?

Ask Janice. Without doing any serious career planning, Janice entered a trade school to become an electrician. She'd heard that electricians made good money. There was a training school near Janice's home. She took the entrance test, passed it, and thought she was on her way to a great career.

Halfway through the course, Janice discovered that she didn't like doing electrical work. She missed talking with people. Connecting wires was boring! Yet she'd spent many months and thousands of dollars on the training. Now Janice has to decide. Should she drop out and start over? Or should she finish what she started?

If you were Janice, what would you do? Why?

A little career planning might have saved Janice time, money, and energy. She could have seen that a career involving contact with people would be more rewarding to her.

Another worker, Jerry, just turned 50. He also just opened his second store. Jerry buys and sells used sports equipment and clothing. His stores are packed with tents, backpacks, skis, down jackets, and more.

In the past, Jerry made a living working as a steamfitter and a shoe repairer. "But now," says Jerry, "for the first time in my life, I feel that I have a real career. I've always liked sports, and I'm very glad to be running my own business. I don't mind working long hours, because I'm doing what I love."

Jerry's only regret is that he didn't start his business sooner. "Perhaps if I'd done some thinking about my values ten years ago, I could have been doing this all along."

Careful career planning can be an exciting process of discovery about yourself and the world you live in. With planning, you are less likely to spend your time doing jobs you don't like. By taking control, you will more quickly reap the rewards that work brings.

Chapter Review

Chapter Summary

- In the United States we have both the freedom and the responsibility of choosing our own careers. We also have the responsibility of preparing for competition in the job market. We must use the resources around us to become our own career managers.

- A career is something you choose. It brings rewards. It is a long-term but not necessarily a lifetime activity. A career can give you the chance to develop your own talents.

- Rewards come in many different forms. Money is one reward, but it is not always the most important one.

- There are seven important steps in planning a career:
1. Looking at the big employment picture. 2. Assessing yourself and your resources. 3. Exploring different careers.
4. Building a foundation for your career with education, experience, and skills. 5. Getting hired. 6. Working at being a success. 7. Making career planning a lifelong process.

- Planning and managing a career has great benefits. It can save you time, energy, and money. It can help you find the work that is the most rewarding to you.

Chapter Quiz

Answer these questions on a separate sheet of paper.

A. Thinking About Careers

1. What is the U.S. job market based on?

2. List three career resources.

3. What are two dictionary definitions of the word "career"?

4. What are three basic needs money can help us answer?

5. What rewards other than money might a career offer?

6. Give an example of how technology has changed the factory as a workplace.

7. What quality can help workers handle change well?

8. Is there a difference between a pay raise and a promotion? Explain.

9. Why is lifelong career planning important?

10. Besides money and energy, what can wise planning help save us?

B. Putting What You Learned to Work

Think of some past accomplishment in your life that you are proud of. It could be an art project, some volunteer work, a first job, or a homework assignment. What made your accomplishment rewarding? Explain.

C. Work Out

Interview an employed person about his or her career. Find out what type of planning he or she did. In your opinion, did the person plan well enough? If so, what makes you think so? If not, how might the person have benefitted from better planning?

Chapter 2
Understanding Employment Trends

Between 1929 and 1940, during the Great Depression, the unemployment rate was very high.

Chapter Learning Objectives

- List and explain four factors that affect employment.
- Name two areas where career opportunities are increasing.
- Name two areas where career opportunities are decreasing.
- Describe the relationship between employment and education.

Words to Know

baby boom   a sudden increase in the birth rate

business cycles   alternating periods of growing and shrinking economic activity

cyclical unemployment   a situation that occurs when people are out of work because of a downturn in the business cycle

demographics   facts or characteristics about a population

diverse   having many different characteristics, varied

goods   things that can be seen, touched, bought, and sold

manufacture   the making of goods with machines, usually in a factory

paralegals   people who assist lawyers

recession   a period when the production of goods and services decreases for six months or more

services   work performed for others, such as teaching or selling

structural unemployment   unemployment that occurs when workers do not have the education or skills to fill available jobs

trend   general direction or tendency

unemployment rate   the percentage of people in the labor force who are looking for work but have not found jobs

Grace Lu and Michael Brown were in their sophomore year of high school.

After school one day, they began to talk about their futures.

"I don't know," Grace said. "All I hear on the news are stories about high unemployment. The future doesn't look too good to me."

"I know what you mean," Michael replied. "My brother managed to get a pretty good job after high school, though."

"What does he do?" Grace asked.

"It has something to do with computers," Michael said. "He always liked fiddling around with electronics. Anyway, he says it's a growing field."

"A growing field! Everybody keeps telling me there are no jobs."

"I don't know," said Michael. "My brother says you have to make your own future."

"Yes, well your brother always was a know-it-all," Grace smiled. "Cute, too."

Michael laughed. "Well, maybe it's time we learned something from him. The next time he's home, I'll ask him how he knew where the jobs were. Maybe he's got some ideas on how to make the future a little brighter."

The Big Picture of Employment

The news often contains employment stories about companies closing and people being laid off work. It can be very discouraging to anyone planning a career.

Michael's brother looked beyond the bad news. He did some research and learned where the jobs were. He was then able to match his skills to a field where there were a growing number of jobs.

This chapter looks at "the big picture" of employment in the United States. In it, you will learn about the kinds of things that affect employment and employment trends. As Michael's brother did, you can use such information to become informed and to prepare yourself for the future.

What Affects Employment?

The *labor force* refers to those 16 years old or older who are either employed or looking for work.

Stop anyone on the street. Ask that person how well he or she thinks the country is doing. Chances are, the person will bring up the unemployment rate. The **unemployment rate** is the percentage of people in the labor force who are looking for work but have not found jobs. If unemployment is down, the person will probably say the country is doing well. If unemployment is up, things might not seem so great.

In this chapter, you will read about four important factors which may affect overall employment and employment trends:

- the demand for goods and services
- international events
- technology
- the population

The Demand for Goods and Services

Every country produces goods and services. **Goods** are things you can see, touch, buy, and sell. Clothing and food are examples of goods. A **service** is any work that a person does for others for money. Salespersons, doctors, and basketball players all provide services.

In the United States, businesses decide which goods and services to produce. Business decisions are based on what people will buy and how much they will pay. This demand directly affects the number and types of jobs available.

Here is an example. Over the last 30 years, travel has become easier and less expensive. As a result, more people are willing and able to travel. This creates a demand for more travel services. If the **trend** continues, there will be more jobs for travel agents in the future.

Of course, nothing is quite that simple. In the American economy, demand, production, and employment go through **business cycles**. Over the period of a cycle, the economy grows for a period of time and then shrinks for a period of time. Here's how it works:

A long, severe recession is called a *depression*. The highest unemployment rate in the United States was in 1932 during the Great Depression. Unemployment skyrocketed to almost 24 percent.

When people can spend more money, businesses produce more for them to buy. In order to produce more, businesses employ more workers. During these times, the economy is growing. This growth hits a peak, and then demand starts to slow. People spend less. Businesses produce less. Fewer workers are needed. **Cyclical unemployment** occurs during this downturn in the business cycle. If the downturn lasts six months or longer, the economy is said to be in a **recession**.

Careers Practice

Answer these questions on a separate sheet of paper.

1. Explain the difference between goods and services.

2. Suppose you hear on the news that there is a downturn in economic activity. What does this mean in terms of overall employment?

3. What is one occupation that might experience seasonal unemployment?

International Events

International events can also greatly affect overall employment. In fact, an international event was responsible for the lowest-ever unemployment rate in this country. In 1944, World War II was raging across the sea. In the United States, the production of wartime equipment was way up. In addition, the labor force was small. Many of the young men who normally would have been working in factories were in the armed forces instead. As a result, the unemployment rate dropped to 1.2 percent.

Trade agreements and foreign competition can also affect employment. For example, in the early 1970s the price of foreign oil dropped. In turn, the United States began importing more oil. This caused many oil workers in the United States to lose their jobs.

Technology

Technology has made it possible to produce goods and services faster. It has given us better health care. It has allowed us to find out what is happening on the other side of the world in seconds. However, as technology plays a larger role in our lives, the number of jobs in some fields will shrink or disappear altogether. The best example of this is in **manufacturing**. In 1979, about 21 million Americans held manufacturing jobs. The current trend shows manufacturing jobs decreasing. According to one estimate, the number of manufacturing jobs will shrink to 600,000 by the year 2005.

Of course, technology also creates jobs. The field of computer programming, for example, has boomed in the last 20 years. Workers must often learn new skills to do new jobs. When workers do not have the skills, there is **structural unemployment**. Structural unemployment is usually more serious and longer-lasting than cyclical unemployment.

The Population

Facts or characteristics about a population, such as age, sex, and patterns of employment, are called **demographics**. By studying a population's demographics, we can better predict where the new jobs will be. For example, after World War II there was a **baby boom** in this country. The birth rate went up 50 percent. A large part of the current U.S. population was born in the 1950s. As these "baby boomers" get older, they will demand more health

Can you think of a job that was created by technology?

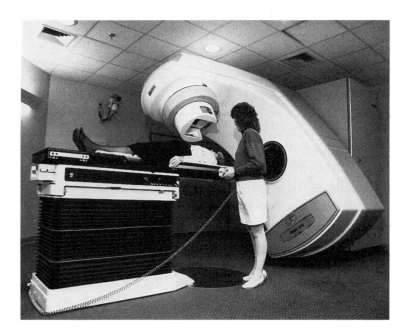

New technology and an aging population mean more jobs in health care.

care services. This is one of the reasons why jobs in the health care industry are growing.

In general, the work force of the future will be more **diverse**. The number of women in the work force will continue to grow. About one quarter of the American work force will be made up of African Americans and Latinos.

Careers Practice

Answers these questions on a separate sheet of paper.

1. Give an example of technology creating a new job field.

2. What is happening to the number of manufacturing jobs?

3. Give an example of how the baby boom may affect employment in the year 2000.

Five Major Employment Trends

Every two years, the Department of Labor looks at trends in U.S. employment. These trends are *best guesses* about what will happen. They can be changed by changes in the demand for goods and services, international events, technology, and the population.

Being aware of trends can help you be realistic about job competition. It also can help you prepare yourself with skills and education. However, you should *not* choose a career based only on trends. Your interests, skills, talents, and abilities are also important.

As you read about these trends, remember that many factors affect employment. Also, these trends are a look at what is happening in the United States as a whole. The trends where you live might be different.

Here are five of the major trends expected to continue between now and the year 2005:

1. *Overall, the American economy is expected to keep growing.*

If the economy grows at a steady pace, the number of jobs should grow by about 19 percent. Roughly 1.5 million new jobs will be created each year.

2. *The greatest number of jobs will be in service occupations.*

Overall, this category of jobs is expected to grow 29 percent, from 19 million to almost 25 million jobs. Police officers, dental assistants, fast-food workers, and barbers are all examples of people with service jobs.

3. *The fastest-growing occupations are in the technical field.*

Technology is rapidly changing. It is no wonder that there will be a demand for people who can work with the new equipment being created. Many of the technical jobs will be health-related. For example, emergency medical technicians will be in high demand. These people will have to know how to operate the latest lifesaving equipment on ambulances.

People with technical jobs don't always work with machines. For instance, the fastest-growing group in the technical category is **paralegals**. Paralegals help lawyers. Among other things, they do research and handle a lot of paperwork. In the coming years, lawyers are expected to rely more and more on paralegals.

4. Fewer jobs will be available in agriculture, forestry, fishing, mining, and manufacturing.

Technology will be responsible for much of the decline in these areas. Farms in the United States will continue to produce great amounts of food. However, with improved equipment, it will take fewer people to produce it. The same thing is happening in mining and manufacturing.

5. To get better-paying jobs, workers of the future will need to be better skilled and better educated.

This is a very important trend. On average, workers who have the most education will earn the most per year. They will also experience less unemployment. This trend does *not* mean that everyone must have four years of college to get a job. High school graduates with solid math, language, and problem-solving skills should be able to find jobs with good pay. There will be service jobs for those who do not have those skills, too. However, these jobs will pay less on average than jobs in other fields.

You and Employment Trends

Again, these trends are just one piece of your career puzzle. You must also explore your interests and abilities. You must look more closely at specific fields and careers. Then you must make your choice. Studying trends can help you with your decision, but they are only one factor to consider.

Careers Practice

Use the graph to answer these questions. Write your answers on a separate sheet of paper.

1. What is the average yearly pay of a person with fewer than four years of high school?

2. What is the average yearly pay of someone with four years of high school?

3. As the number of years of education increases, what else increases?

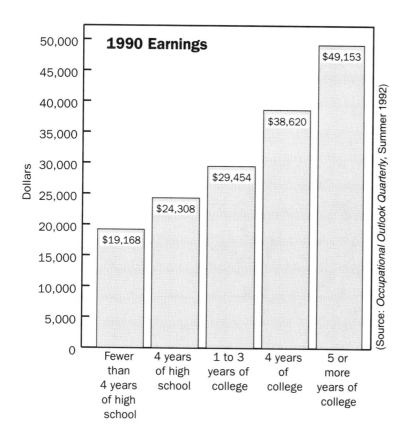

1990 Earnings

(Source: Occupational Outlook Quarterly, Summer 1992)

It's History

Are you thinking about becoming a robot repairer? Perhaps you'd like a career as a "computer detective." This person tracks down people who use computers to steal information or money.

If you are considering any career in electronics, you can thank the *transistor*. The transistor is a very small device that controls the flow of electric current. It was first used in radios and televisions in the 1950s. Now we find transistors in hearing aids, stereos, calculators, and computers.

Just how small is a transistor? The average personal computer runs on a silicon chip that is about a quarter of an inch square. This chip is called a *microprocessor*. It can contain up to 6,000 transistors!

The transistor and the microprocessor have changed the way people work all over the world. They are responsible for many new jobs in the electronics industry.

Chapter Review

Chapter Summary

- Employment and employment trends are affected by four major factors. They are the demand for goods and services, international events, technology, and the population.

- When the demand for goods and services is high, the economy is growing. Employment is usually up. When the demand decreases, so does production. Employment goes down. This downturn in the business cycle results in *cyclical unemployment*.

- International events that affect U.S. employment include war, trade agreements, and competition.

- Technology creates some jobs and eliminates others.

- Characteristics of the population, called *demographics,* also shape employment trends. Now that the large "baby boom" generation is growing older, there will be greater employment opportunities in the health care field.

- Overall, the American economy is expected to continue growing. By the year 2005, the greatest number of jobs will be in service occupations. Many jobs should become available in technical fields. As a rule, fewer jobs will be available in agriculture, forestry, fishing, mining, and manufacturing.

- Workers of the future will need to be better skilled and better educated. This will largely be due to new and better technology in the workplace.

Chapter Quiz

Answer these questions on a separate sheet of paper.

A. Thinking About Careers

1. If people have little money to spend, is the demand for goods and services likely to be high or low?

2. If the demand for goods and services rises, what is likely to happen to the number of available jobs?

3. If a downturn in the economy lasts more than six months, what is it called?

4. When does structural unemployment occur?

5. Give an example of how international events can affect employment.

6. What is one reason why the number of health care jobs is expected to grow?

7. Give an example of a technical job.

8. The number of service occupations is growing. Give two examples of service jobs.

9. What is likely to happen to the number of jobs in forestry, fishing, and mining?

10. How can education affect one's chances for employment?

B. Putting What You Learned to Work

Think about the neighborhood where you live. What is the employment trend among people there? Are most people working?

C. Work Out

Suppose a friend tells you he's thinking about dropping out of school. He's tired of not having any money. He says he's ready to get a full-time job. He wants to be able to buy whatever appeals to him. What might you tell your friend about trends in education and employment? Be sure to use figures to support your statements.

Unit One Review

Answer these questions on a separate sheet of paper.

1. What are three needs that can be satisfied by earning money through work?

2. In addition to money, what rewards might an ambulance driver get from working?

3. Why might a company move from one state to another?

4. What can career planning do for you?

5. What caused the lowest unemployment rate in U.S. history?

6. When did the United States experience the highest unemployment rate?

7. When the production of goods and services increases, what happens to employment?

8. The aging population is one reason why the number of health care jobs is likely to increase. What is another reason?

9. Give two examples of demographics that might affect employment trends.

10. Why is it important to get a good education?

Assessing Yourself

Chapter 3

Assessing Your Strengths

It is sometimes easier to measure physical strengths than career strengths.

Chapter Learning Objectives

- Explain why it is important to know your strengths.
- List four assessment resources.
- Explain the differences between interests, skills, and personality traits.
- Describe a personal accomplishment and the strengths related to it.

Words to Know

accomplishment   a successfully completed task; an achievement

analyze   to examine closely

aptitude   a natural ability to learn or do something well

assess   to judge or set a value on

career counselor   a trained professional who helps people with their career searches

data   information

interests   things a person is curious about or likes to do

personality traits   the ways a person behaves; characteristics

self-esteem   self-respect

skill   an ability to do something well

strategy   a plan

transferable   easily moved or exchanged from one place to another

---

In his junior year of high school, Ken decided to look for a part-time job. Before beginning his job search, he talked to his girlfriend Jean.

"I could apply at Burger Hut," Ken said, "but I don't want just any job. I want to enjoy my work. I want to work at a job that I'll be good at. I just don't have any idea what that job might be."

Jean thought for a moment. "Well," she said, "start by looking at what you already do well. You play sports well. You're friendly. People feel comfortable around you."

Ken blushed. "Do you really think so?"

Jean laughed. "Don't take my word for it. Stop and think about yourself. What do you think you do well?"

"Well, I'm pretty good at math."

Jean nodded her head. "Say, maybe you should try for a sales job in a sports equipment store. You know about sports equipment. People like to talk to you. You could add up the sales without a problem. It might be a perfect job for you."

What other work might Ken be suited to do?

Ken hugged Jean. "You're pretty smart," he told her. "I think I know a good job for you, too."

"What's that?"

"I think you would make a great **career counselor**."

Why You Must Assess Your Strengths

Ken is taking a look at the things he likes to do and the things he does well. He is exploring his interests and his skills. In short, he is **assessing** his strengths and trying to match them to a job.

To be able to choose a career that suits you, you should assess your strengths. Successful people choose work that allows them to put their strengths to good use. You may find that the things you most like to do and the things you do best are often the same.

Assessing your strengths can help you in another way. Employers hire workers because their strengths will help their companies. People who can talk about their strengths during job interviews have better chances of being hired.

Looking at your strengths is also a good way to boost your **self-esteem** or self-respect. People with high self-esteem are confident. They feel good about themselves. High self-esteem comes across in job interviews. Employers see it as a positive trait.

People with high self-esteem do not always find the jobs they want right away. However, they do recover from disappointment. Then they get on with their job search.

Assessment Resources

Taking a good look at who you are may be a new process for you. Luckily, there are several good resources to help you.

1. Books

Later in this chapter, you will do a self-assessment. You will work on your own to uncover your strengths.

This book, and other career books in stores and libraries, are important tools. They walk you through the steps of self-assessment. Completing these steps takes some time and energy. However, it is often a wonderful process of self-discovery. Learning to say, "Hey, I'm good at this!" can make any person's day a little better.

2. Family and friends

To do a good self-assessment of your strengths, you must be honest and fair. Sometimes we feel uncomfortable saying or even just thinking about what we do well. At other times, we may think we're better at something than we really are. For this reason, trusted family members and friends are also good resources. They can point out strengths we may not be aware of. This is what Jean did for Ken at the beginning of this chapter.

3. Career counselors

Career counselors help match people with the right careers. They are trained in assessing a person's strengths. They can suggest different fields where these strengths can be put to use.

If you choose to work with a counselor, remember that the two of you form a team. The counselor can ask good questions and give you helpful information. However, your time, energy, and honesty are still required. In the end, any career decisions are up to you.

Where do you find a career counselor? Quite often, schools have counselors who can help you. If there is no counselor in your school, a teacher may be able to direct you to counselors in your community. You can also look in the phone book under *Careers*.

One of the most popular career books is *What Color Is Your Parachute?* by Richard Nelson Bolles. It contains many self-assessment exercises for career hunters.

Talk over your strengths with family members and friends you trust.

Mechanics, music, art, writing, and sports are just a few areas where people have aptitudes. What do you have an aptitude for?

Be sure to ask whomever you are thinking of working with about fees. Many counselors charge a lot of money for their services. Some charge little or nothing. The amount is no guarantee of success or failure. Try to get the recommendation of someone you trust before deciding on whom you will ask for help.

4. Assessment tests

Assessment tests are often used by career counselors to help people discover their strengths. Such tests, however, are not the kind you pass or fail. Their purpose is to help pinpoint your interests and strengths.

One set of assessment tests is the General Aptitude Test Battery (GATB). It measures a person's **aptitude**, or natural ability to do well in various areas. For example, some people have an aptitude for learning math. They add, subtract, and perform other math activities more easily than most people do.

A career counselor or some other trained person can show you how to complete these tests. A trained person must also help you understand your test results.

Careers Practice

Answer these questions on a separate sheet of paper.

1. Give one reason for assessing your strengths.

2. Explain how your family and friends can be an important assessment resource.

3. What does the word "aptitude" mean?

How to Begin a Self-Assessment

When young people begin self-assessments, they often say, "I've never held a job. I don't have any real strengths."

Most of us do have strengths, though. We just have to know how to recognize them. As you read earlier, there are many career books that can walk you through the steps of self-assessment. Here, however, is a common method to help you get started right now.

Begin by listing your accomplishments. An **accomplishment** is something you have done well. Here are some examples:

- Won a tennis match.
- Wrote a poem.
- Received a B on a history test.
- Decorated your bedroom.
- Got a part in the school play.
- Worked as a recreation assistant with the Parks Department.

Tell a friend about one of your accomplishments. Get used to talking about what you do well.

It doesn't matter how small the accomplishment was. Just write down as many accomplishments as you can think of. A list of ten is a good start.

Interests Are Also Strengths

Look at your list of accomplishments. This should help you see what your **interests** are. The two may be very closely linked. An interest is something you are curious about or like to do. You might have an interest in sports, music, art, computers, animals, children, clothes, books, or food. There are as many interests in the world as there are people and things!

List your interests and then think carefully about them. Which do you feel strongly about? If you had to make choices, which ones would you choose? Ranking your interests can help you decide which you would like to spend the most time on.

Later, you can link these interests to possible careers. For example, you may have an interest in animals and an interest in computers. Dogs are nice as pets, you think, but you wouldn't want a career as an animal trainer. Your interest in computers far outweighs your interest in animals. You would take this difference into account when choosing a future career.

Hard and Soft Skills

Certain accomplishments require certain **skills**. Skills can generally be placed into one of two groups: hard skills and soft skills.

Hard skills are those that are related to specific jobs or tasks. For example, typing is a hard skill. Operating a cash register is a hard skill. So is operating a forklift. Employers often look for people with hard skills to

Are you interested enough in animals to become an animal trainer?

perform certain jobs. This saves them the time and cost of training new workers.

Think back to Ken's situation at the beginning of this chapter. Suppose one of his accomplishments was winning a city tennis tournament. Ken could list his forehand and backhand strokes as hard skills. It would be necessary for a tennis coach to have these hard skills. They would not be useful in a job at Burger Hut.

Soft skills are those that can be used on almost any job. For example, some people have what the Irish call "the gift of gab." They talk easily to people. For the most part, people enjoy listening to them. Such people have spoken communication skills. These skills can help a person do just about any job. Because of this, they are sometimes called **transferable** skills.

Learn More About It: DOT Skills

The *Dictionary of Occupational Titles* (DOT) is a book published by the U.S. Department of Labor. The DOT includes descriptions of many different jobs and the skills required for each.

The DOT divides all skills into three categories: data, people, and things. **Data** skills involve working with information, such as statistics or reports. People skills can be used with anyone in the world of work: co-workers, bosses, and customers, for example. The third category, things, has to do with machines and materials. Here are examples of some skills in each of these categories:

Data	People	Things
analyzing	instructing	driving
computing	serving	handling
comparing	speaking	operating
coordinating	persuading	setting up

Think about your own accomplishments. Then think about the skills you've used. Have you tended to work with data, people, or things?

In Ken's case, he had to plan a **strategy** to win each game in the city tennis tournament. He looked carefully at the way each person played. Then he adjusted his own style in order to be able to beat them. Ken has the soft skills of **analyzing** and coming up with strategies. These skills can be used in many different jobs—even at Burger Hut.

How might Ken use his strategy-planning skills at a food service job?

Careers Practice

Answer these questions on a separate sheet of paper.

1. Suppose that Polly writes a story for the school newspaper. She interviews a teacher and writes the story on a personal computer. She uses a computer program called "Write-Right." What is one of Polly's hard skills?

2. What is one of Polly's soft skills?

Your Personality Is a Strength

Your **personality traits**, or characteristics, are also strengths. Some examples of personality traits are loyalty, calmness, and curiosity.

Some personality traits show up at birth. Some babies are fussy, others quiet. Some smile a lot, others cry easily. Personality traits are shaped by experience. A young girl who is rewarded for outgoing behavior will tend to repeat that behavior. If she is punished for being outgoing, she may become withdrawn. Your personality is something that does not change easily. However, it can change over time.

Career counselors can help you define your personality traits. You can also link your personality traits to your accomplishments. When Ken won the tennis tournament, he showed he was competitive. This could serve him well as a salesperson.

Some Personality Traits

Read this list of personality traits. Which could you use to describe yourself?

accurate	direct	steady
adventurous	emotional	supportive
analytical	forceful	risk taker
calm	loyal	team player
charming	outgoing	unselfish
dependable	sensitive	well-disciplined

Your Developing Strengths

By now you should be developing an idea of what our own strengths are. If you haven't already done so, begin listing them. Add to the list as you become aware of your strengths. Think, too, about which skills you want to continue using. In coming chapters, you will see how to match your strengths to a career. You will also see how to use your strengths when writing résumés and going on job interviews.

Which of your strengths do you want to make the most use of?

Make a practice of thinking about your daily accomplishments. Write them down. Some will be small, such as learning to operate a copy machine. Others, such as graduating from high school, will be the result of long, hard work. With each new accomplishment, think about the interests, skills, and personality traits that could be related to it. Knowing yourself and your strengths is an important step in your career search.

Chapter Review

Chapter Summary

- To find a career you will enjoy doing and be successful in, assess your strengths. Then match them to a career.

- Knowing your strengths will boost your self-esteem. It can also help you write résumés and interview for jobs.

- There are many resources to help you assess your strengths. They include career books, your family and friends, career counselors, and assessment tests.

- Listing your accomplishments is a good way to start a self-assessment. Then you can pinpoint the interests, skills, and personality traits that made your accomplishments possible.

- Hard skills are task-related. They help a person do specific jobs. Typing and operating a computer are examples of hard skills.

- Soft skills are transferable from one job to another. Speaking and writing are soft skills.

- Your interests, skills, and personality traits may change some-what over time. Knowing which strengths you want to continue using and developing will help you steer toward rewarding career goals.

Chapter Quiz

Answer these questions on a separate sheet of paper.

A. Thinking About Careers

1. Why is it important to assess your strengths?

2. Where can you find books useful in self-assessments?

3. How can family and friends help you assess your strengths?

4. Where is one place to find a career counselor?

5. What might an assessment test such as the GATB measure?

6. What is a common first step in doing a self-assessment?

7. Jean lists baking a cake from scratch as an accomplishment. What is one of her interests?

8. Jean used an electric mixer to make the cake. Is this a hard or soft skill?

9. Jean followed instructions to make the cake. Is this a hard or soft skill?

10. Give an example of three personality traits that could be considered strengths.

B. Putting What You Learned to Work

Describe the interests, skills, and personality traits that led to one of your accomplishments.

C. Work Out

Choose a job or career that you know something about. Describe at least three strengths that you think a person in that job should have.

Chapter 4

Making Lifestyle Choices

Would an airline attendant's lifestyle appeal to you?

Chapter Learning Objectives

- Explain how lifestyle choices are linked to career choices.
- List personal values in order of importance.
- Name five lifestyle factors.
- Describe how tradeoffs work when making lifestyle choices.

Words to Know

apprenticeship an on-the-job training program in which a skilled worker teaches someone a trade or craft

attendant a person who serves or helps another

environment all the things that surround and affect a person

executive a person who helps run a business

job sharing a situation in which two people share the responsibilities of a single job

leisure free time used for rest or recreation

prioritize to rank in order of importance

temporary agency an agency that finds temporary jobs for workers

vocational school a school that trains people to do specific jobs or trades

It was Career Day at Sumner High School. Marcus and Julia were listening to Mr. Piper, an airline **attendant**, talk about his job.

"I have the cross-country route," Mr. Piper explained. "That means I fly from New York to Los Angeles several times per week. I share an apartment in each city with friends. On the plane, I spend much of my time serving food and drinks to the passengers. Often, I have to calm people who are nervous about flying. Sometimes, I have to clean up after them when they get sick."

"Yuck," whispered Marcus.

"Most of the time," the speaker continued, "I enjoy my work. I love the people I meet, and I love traveling. Because I work for an airline, I get discounts on plane tickets. On my vacation, I can fly almost anywhere for a very low cost—sometimes for free!"

Later, Julia and Marcus talked about what they'd heard. "It sounds like a great job," Julia beamed.

"Living in different cities, meeting new people all the time. How exciting!"

Marcus looked doubtful. "I don't know," he said. "I've been thinking that after getting a job I'd still live at home. I want to help raise my brother and sister. Plus, I don't think I'd like being cooped up in a plane all the time. I need fresh air. I'd probably be one of those people who gets sick to his stomach! I don't think being an airline attendant would fit the lifestyle I want."

Lifestyle Choices and Career Choices

In Chapter 3, you read about how important it is to assess your strengths. By matching your interests, skills, and personality traits to a career, you'll increase your chances of enjoying your job and doing it well.

Now you must think about the lifestyle you want. Lifestyle choices and career choices go hand-in-hand. Marcus knew he didn't want a job that required him to travel. He wanted to be near his family. Julia, on the other hand, found the airline attendant's lifestyle attractive. She wanted to travel and meet new people.

Values and a Balanced Lifestyle

Making lifestyle choices begins with looking closely at your values. In Chapter 1, you learned that values are the principles a person holds to be important. They are that person's standards or beliefs. For instance, Jane is a young mother. She has a three-year-old child. Jane's most important value is being a good mother. However, she also wants to have a career in fashion. This is important to her. In addition, she enjoys reading. Jane has a part-time sales job in a store where she can keep up on the latest clothing designs. She spends the rest of the time raising her child. In

Working parents must balance the need to be with their children with the need to work.

the evenings, she tries to take at least 30 minutes to do some reading. She feels her life has balance. This helps her stay happy.

There are as many values and lifestyle choices as there are people. Your best friend's idea of a balanced lifestyle may be completely different from your own. Values and lifestyle choices change over time, as well. Ask your teacher how he or she used to spend Saturday nights as a teenager. Does your teacher

Your accomplishments, interests, skills, and personality traits are linked to your values.

spend Saturday nights the same way now? Probably not. Values and lifestyles are things you can continue thinking about as you grow older.

The exercise below will help you identify some of your values and prioritize them. When you **prioritize,** you rank items in order of importance. Once you do this, many lifestyle choices should become clearer to you.

I value . . .

being healthy

having lots of
   free time

being part of a
   community

living in a healthy
   environment

making money

being safe

being a leader

having a family

looking fashionable

working as part of
   a group

having a good
   education

helping others

working with people

working with things

working with
   information

being respected

working outdoors

learning new things

working by myself

having a good sense
   of humor

Careers Practice

Answer these questions on a separate sheet of paper.

1. Look at the list of values above. List all of these values that apply to you. Add others if you like.

2. Rank the values in order of their importance to you. The most important will be number 1, the second most important number 2, and so on.

3. Look at your most important value. How might it affect a career decision? Give an example.

Exploring Lifestyle Choices

Perhaps you are asking the question, "How can I choose a lifestyle? I still live at home. I've barely held a job."

For now, all you need is a little experience, desire, and imagination. Have you thought about what kind of car you want to drive? Do you dream of going to Paris? Are you planning to have a family of your own someday? If so, you are already exploring lifestyle choices.

The more you know what it is you want, the better chance you have of choosing a career that will help you get it.

Below are five lifestyle factors to consider when thinking about careers. As you study them, recall your interests, skills, personality traits, and values. You may find that making lifestyle choices is a fun exercise!

Factor 1: Consider Location

Some people want to live near their families. Others can't wait to move away. People who like to windsurf want to live near an ocean or other large body of water—not in the middle of a prairie.

Would you consider working in a different country?

Right now, you may be able to apply for jobs close to where you live. As you grow older and become more independent, you may become eager to explore other parts of the world. It is also possible that your career will *require* you to move away.

Think carefully about the way in which *where* you live will affect *how* you live.

- Do I prefer to live in a city, a town, the suburbs, or the country?
- Am I willing to commute to work? If so, how many miles am I willing to travel each day?
- Do I want to be close to mountains, oceans, rivers, or forests?
- What climates do I like?
- Do I want to live near my family and friends?
- Would I like to live in a different culture?
- What kinds of cultural or athletic resources do I want to be near?

Factor 2: Consider the Work Environment

Your work **environment** includes the building you work in, the people you work with, the type of work you do, and more. Quite often, people choose jobs or careers based on *what* they will be doing. *Where* they will be working may be just as important, however. Sarah, for example, took a summer job selling hot dogs at a ballpark. She loved the noise, the crowds, and the fresh air. Juan preferred to take a summer job reshelving books in a library. He liked the quiet, the books, and working independently. Each found a work environment that suited them perfectly.

Take a moment to think about your ideal work environment.

- Would I like sitting for long periods at a desk?
- Would I like working for long periods with a computer?
- Does it matter to me if there are windows where I work?
- Can I work where it is noisy?
- How would I feel about working outside in cold or rainy weather?
- Would I like a job that would require me to wear a uniform or a suit every day?
- Would I like going to meetings?
- How would I feel about a supervisor checking my work?
- Would I like to have people bringing me problems to solve?

Which work environment appeals to you more, a ballpark or a library? Why?

Factor 3: Consider Time Requirements

It was once common for most working people in the United States to work six days a week, twelve hours a day. Today we value our **leisure** time much more than people did then. We want our careers to accommodate our outside interests. A police officer, for example, may try to keep from working the night shift so that he can attend band practice three nights a week.

These days, people have more options than ever before when it comes to time and work. There are full-time, three-quarter time, and half-time jobs. **Temporary agencies** help people find jobs that last days, weeks, or months. People who want complete control of their time sometimes start their own businesses. (Working for yourself, however, often means working much longer and harder than working for others.)

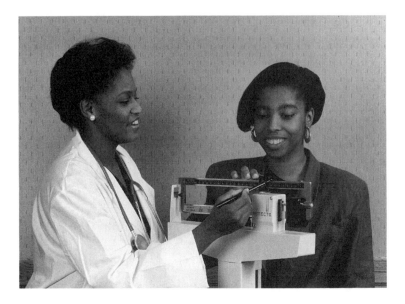

What would a nurse's work environment include?

Think about these questions when considering time requirements:

- Would I be willing to work night or overnight shifts?
- Would I be willing to work weekends?
- Would I mind being on call for emergencies?
- Do I want full-time or part-time work?
- How much vacation time would I like each year?
- Do I want to work for a temporary agency?
- Would I be willing to spend long hours running my own business?

Careers Practice

Answer these questions on a separate sheet of paper.

1. Where might you look for a job if you wanted to live in a warm climate?

2. Suppose you worked in a school office. What are three things you might find in your work environment?

3. What kind of time requirements might a musician's job require?

Making It Work: Job Sharing in the 1990s

In 1991, almost 60 percent of the mothers in the work force had children under the age of six. How do they balance the need for a career and income with the responsibilities of being a mother?

One way is through job sharing. **Job sharing** means that two or more employees share the responsibilities of a particular job. They meet regularly to coordinate their shared tasks.

More and more companies are allowing working parents to job share. One survey shows that employees who shared jobs had higher overall job satisfaction.

Job sharing is not for everyone. It requires flexibility and the ability to communicate well.

Does job sharing sound like one way to meet your lifestyle requirements?

Factor 4: Consider Training and Education

In Chapter 2, you read that education can increase the likelihood of finding employment. Often, the more education a person has, the more money he or she will earn.

However, not everyone wants to or is able to go to a four-year college. Some people are more suited to **apprenticeships** or other on-the-job training programs. Other people will want to go to **vocational schools** to learn certain skills. Community colleges sometimes offer the lowest-priced job training.

Before choosing a career, know what you are willing to do in terms of education and training. Ask yourself these questions:

- Would I be willing to take evening classes? How often and for how long?
- Am I willing to spend time in a training school or in college?
- Can I afford to pay for further education and training beyond high school?
- Am I willing to participate in on-the-job training if it means lower pay while I'm being trained?
- Am I willing to give up time with my family and friends while developing my skills?

Factor 5: Consider Income

This is an easy one, right? Just about everyone wants to make a lot of money. Perhaps, but not everyone is willing to work hard to get it. Highly paid **executives** may work 80-hour weeks and worry constantly about business. Sometimes, they work hard for years before "making it."

Most of us want the basic "American dream." We want a nice place to live, good food, stylish clothes, and money for extras. When thinking about your income, be realistic. Ask yourself these questions:

- What is the minimum amount of money I must make?
- What is the *ideal* amount of money I want to make?
- Am I willing to start at low pay with the promise of higher income later?
- Would I be willing to start at a good pay rate but without the chance to earn more?

Making Choices: A Question of Tradeoffs

Shelly, a high school student, answered all the questions in this chapter. She thought carefully about her values and lifestyles. She then decided that she'd like a career as a lifeguard in Hawaii. She also wants a big house, a great stereo, and $50,000 per year.

When Shelly looked into the career of lifeguarding, she was disappointed. At best, she'll make $10 per hour. Housing in Hawaii is quite expensive. However, Shelly will be able to share an apartment with friends. As for the stereo, she might have to settle for a portable tape player and a set of earphones.

Shelly will have to trade off one thing to get another. She may decide that lifeguarding in Hawaii is more important to her than $50,000 per year. She may also decide to explore a career that would allow her to earn that much.

Did Shelly waste her time by exploring an ideal lifestyle? Not at all. Whatever decision she now makes, she'll feel better knowing what she's giving up and what she's getting.

In Units Three and Four, you will explore different careers. It may be that you will find the ideal career to suit your strengths, values, *and* chosen lifestyle. More likely, you will find that you have to make some tradeoffs. Like Shelly, you should be able to make career decisions that will help keep your life balanced and happy. That is what is really important.

Chapter Review

Chapter Summary

- Lifestyle and career choices go hand-in-hand. One greatly affects the other. Deciding on the type of life you want to lead will help you select a rewarding career.

- Identifying your values will help you make realistic lifestyle choices.

- Assessing your lifestyle choices is a lifelong process, just as career planning is.

- There are at least five important lifestyle factors to consider when thinking about a career. They are location, work environment, time requirements, education and training, and income. Each requires careful thought.

- It is rare for people to find careers that match all their requirements. Often, they trade off one thing, such as a large income, for another, such as a healthy work environment.

Chapter Quiz

Answer these questions on a separate sheet of paper.

A. Thinking About Careers

1. What is one lifestyle choice an airline attendant would make?

2. What is a vocational school?

3. What does it mean to prioritize values?

4. Give an example of a value.

5. Why should you continue to examine your lifestyle choices throughout your life?

6. What is one thing to consider when choosing an area in which to work and live?

7. What is one thing to consider when choosing a work environment?

8. What are two ways in which workers might arrange the time they spend working?

9. What are two ways to get education or training for a career or job?

10. Give an example of a lifestyle choice involving a tradeoff.

B. Putting What You Learned to Work

Select one of the five lifestyle factors described in this chapter. Answer all the questions that are listed under that factor. Explain your answer to another student in your class.

C. Work Out

Many companies and government agencies are making it illegal to smoke cigarettes in the workplace. Do you think such policies are a good idea? Why or why not? How might they affect a person's career choices?

Unit Two Review

Answer these questions on a separate sheet of paper.

1. Most people want careers they enjoy and are successful in. To find such a career, what must you first assess?

2. Knowing your strengths can help boost your self-esteem. What is self-esteem?

3. What are three resources that can be helpful in assessing your strengths?

4. Interests, skills, and personality traits are all examples of what?

5. A good way to begin assessing your strengths is to list the things you have completed and are proud of. What are these things called?

6. Why is it important to think about your lifestyle before choosing a career?

7. To make lifestyle choices, what must you first be aware of?

8. How old must you be before you can choose a lifestyle?

9. What are three factors to consider when choosing a lifestyle?

10. After you assess your strengths and lifestyle choices, what are you ready to do?

Unit Three

Exploring Careers

Chapter 5

How to Explore a Career

Photojournalists sometimes have to face danger to get just the right photograph.

Chapter Learning Objectives

- List three ways to explore careers.
- Describe three books often used to explore careers.
- Explain when and how to do informational interviews.
- List questions asked in informational interviews.

Words to Know

appointment   an arrangement to meet at a certain time and place

counselor   one who listens and offers ideas

informational interview   a question-and-answer session between a person who is exploring a career and a person who has that career

performing arts   activities done in front of an audience, such as acting or playing music

photojournalist   a person who takes photographs for newspapers and magazines

professional association   an organization whose members all have the same occupation. Members of professional associations usually meet regularly to share information.

research   careful study

visual arts   activities such as painting, drawing, sculpting, and photography

---

Roberta and Marilyn walked to their lockers after the last class of the day.

"I'm hungry," said Marilyn. "Let's get something to eat before we walk home."

"It sounds good, but I can't," Roberta answered. "I'm going to see Mr. Lee."

Marilyn look surprised. "Really? The journalism teacher? You're not in his class. Did you get in trouble with him or something?"

Roberta opened her locker. "No. I told Mr. Lee that I might like a career as a **photojournalist**. I'd take pictures for newspapers. Mr. Lee has a friend who does this. He's going to give me his friend's phone number. He's also going to help me prepare questions to ask his friend."

Marilyn thought for a minute. "How do you know that you want to be a photojournalist?"

Roberta began walking down the hall. "I did some reading about it. Actually, I'm not 100 percent sure it is what I want to be. Talking to Mr. Lee's friend will help me make up my mind."

Marilyn watched her friend walk away. She thought it was about time for her to begin exploring careers, too.

Ways to Explore a Career

When you have outlined your accomplishments and assessed your strengths, think about the lifestyle you want. Now you're ready to explore careers. Roberta, for example, had taken photographs for the high school yearbook. She had learned to use a camera and counted this as one of her skills. Roberta enjoyed using her creativity. She also liked seeing her work in print. So Roberta decided to explore a career as a photographer. She wanted to learn as much about this career as possible. Then she could make a decision about whether it was right for her.

How do you learn about a career without actually doing it? You can:

- Talk to a career **counselor**.
- Read about the career.
- Talk to someone who works in the field you're interested in. This is called doing an **informational interview**.

Does your school have a career center? If not, ask a teacher or librarian about free or low-cost career centers in your city. Career centers are often found in libraries.

As you know, career counselors are trained to help you find a career. They can point you in the direction of jobs that may match your interests, skills, and personality traits. However, career counselors can only direct you. They cannot make your decisions for you. It is a good idea to do your own **research**. You may find some things that the career counselor might miss. A good first step is to read about careers and what they offer.

Reading About Careers

Career centers, and most libraries, are full of career information. They have books, articles, and sometimes videos about work. They may also have job listings.

One of the most useful books for young people is the *Guide to Occupational Exploration* (GOE). The GOE is put out by the U.S. Department of Labor. It lists 12 main interest areas and the careers that suit people with those interests. It also includes helpful information and questions to help you narrow your career search.

Roberta used the GOE in her career exploration. After she outlined her accomplishments, she saw that her interests and skills were mainly in the arts. Roberta liked drawing, painting, and photography. She felt she was creative and adventurous, but she didn't know what career she wanted.

Roberta opened the GOE to the table of contents. There she saw "artistic" as the first interest area listed. Under artistic were several smaller groups, such as **visual arts** and **performing arts**: music. Roberta turned to the visual arts section and learned that drawing, painting, and photography were in this category. She then found information about careers in visual arts. The book asked—and helped her answer—these questions:

- What kind of work would you do in the visual arts field?
- What skills and abilities do you need for this kind of work?
- How do you know if you would like or could learn to do this kind of work?
- How can you prepare for and enter this field?
- What else should you consider about these jobs?

The GOE listed 51 job titles that might suit a person who wanted a career in visual arts. From those 51,

Roberta picked five to look at more closely. Three of them involved photography.

Careers Practice

Answer these questions on a separate sheet of paper.

1. What resources are found in career centers and libraries?

2. What does GOE stand for?

3. What is one of the interest areas in the GOE?

More Reading about Careers

Another commonly used career exploration book is the *Dictionary of Occupational Titles* (DOT). The DOT has short descriptions of more than 20,000 job titles! Career explorers can scan the occupational categories, divisions, and groups to find particular job areas. They can also look up job titles in the index. For example, Roberta could have looked up Occupations in Photography. In the index, she could have looked up the job title *photojournalist*.

Another well-known resource is the *Occupational Outlook Handbook* (OOH). The Bureau of Labor Statistics publishes this book every two years. In it, you can find up-to-date information about trends in over 250 occupations. Some 87 percent of all the jobs in the United States fall into the occupations covered in the OOH.

The OOH puts occupations into 13 large clusters. These clusters are divided into smaller occupational groups. It's a good idea to look over the OOH table of contents completely for occupations you want to explore. Health-related jobs, for example, can be found in four of the clusters.

Do you know what a *roustabout* does? How about an *offal separator*? Look them up in the DOT to find out!

The *Occupational Outlook Quarterly* provides an update to the OOH. The update is published every three months. Look in the Quarterly for the most current employment trends.

The OOH lists information under these key headings:

- *The nature of the work.* This section includes typical tasks, duties, responsibilities, and equipment used on a job.
- *Working conditions.* These include hours, work setting, and safety concerns, among other things.
- *Employment.* Here you can find how many jobs there were in this field in a recent year. You might also learn in what areas of the country most of the jobs are located. Information on part-time and self-employment might also appear here.
- *Training, other qualifications, and advancement.* Do you want to know what kind of education or training you need to get a job? Is it an entry-level job, the kind for which you don't need a lot of skills in that job area? Or do you need years of education and training? What are your chances of getting ahead? If you want answers to these questions, look under this heading.
- *Job outlook.* Here you can find current information about trends that may affect this occupation. For example, will the number of jobs in this field increase or decrease? Why?
- *Earnings.* Information under this heading tells you how much money you can expect to make. Sometimes it will describe other benefits you may get on a job. For example, if your employer is a hospital, you may get free medical insurance.
- *Related Occupations.* Here you can find other occupations that may interest you.
- *Sources of Additional Information.* This section lists organizations that you can contact for more details.

The GOE, DOT, and OOH are just three of the many books that can help you explore careers. Libraries and career centers have dozens of others. Once you find a certain career, try looking it up in the

Would a career as a photojournalist suit your lifestyle?

OOH Facts about Photojournalists

Nature of Work:

Photojournalists use 35-millimeter cameras to shoot events, places, people, and things. Their photos are used in newspapers and magazines.

Working Conditions:

News photographers may have to travel overnight or to faraway places. At times, they may have to photograph dangerous events such as wars or disasters.

Training, Other Qualifications, and Advancement:

Many photographers are self-taught or learn in apprenticeships. Many newspapers and magazines require their photographers to have formal training in photography. Photojournalists must know how to operate a camera and understand how to get the best photograph for a story. They may someday head the photography department in a newspaper or magazine.

Job Outlook:

Employment in photojournalism is expected to grow slowly. It is a highly competitive field.

Earnings:

In 1990, the average minimum starting salary for a news photographer was $426 per week.

Related Occupations:

Painters, designers

Sources of Additional Information:

Professional Photographers of America, Inc., 1090 Executive Way, Des Plaines, IL 60018.

Source: *Occupational Outlook Handbook*, Bureau of Labor Statistics, 1992

card catalog or magazine index. For example, Roberta could look in her library's card catalog under *photographers* and *photojournalists.* In this way, she would find the titles of books on these subjects.

Careers Practice

Answer these questions on a separate sheet of paper.

1. What does DOT stand for?

2. What will you find in the DOT?

3. What book would you look in to find out how much a welder might earn?

The Informational Interview

At the beginning of this chapter, you read that Roberta was going to interview a photojournalist. During this interview, she planned to ask key questions about the work this person does. This information would help Roberta decide if she really wanted to pursue a career in photojournalism.

Informational interviews are a good way to explore careers. An airplane pilot can tell you what it's like to fly through the clouds. A roofer can tell you what it's like to work 30 feet off the ground every day. A parent can tell you what it's like to listen to a baby cry for four hours straight. This is information that you might not find in a careers book. It is also information that can help you make up your mind.

Interviews will take up not only your time but also the time of the person you interview. Only do interviews when you're serious about a career. Do your research first. In this way you will be asking questions that cannot easily be answered by looking in a book. To make the process worthwhile, follow these key steps:

Only a pilot can tell you what it's like to fly a plane.

1. *Find a person who has the job or career you are interested in.* To do so, you might ask your family, friends, a career counselor, or a teacher. You can also go to **professional associations.** These are organizations whose members all have the same occupation. Members of professional associations usually meet regularly and share information. Quite often, they have programs to help people just beginning in a career. For example, Roberta might have found a professional association for photojournalists in her city. One of the members of that group might have been happy to do an informational interview with her. That person might even have been willing to let Roberta observe the job first-hand.

2. *Call and make an* **appointment** *with the person you want to talk to.* Explain that you want information, not a job. Limit the interview to about 30 minutes.

3. *To prepare, write down your interview questions ahead of time.* Think carefully about what you want to find out. You'll use the information you gather to help you decide whether the job will fit with your strengths and lifestyle choices. Among the questions you might ask are: What are your responsibilities on the job? What kind of training or education do you need for this kind of work? What is a typical day on the job like? What things do you like about your job? What things don't you like? What kinds of income and benefits might I expect in such a job?

4. *Keep your appointment and be on time!* If you cannot make it, be sure to call and ask to reschedule.

5. *Either write down the answers to the questions or tape-record the interview.* You can study the information more carefully later. If you do use a tape recorder, you should still keep a notebook handy. This will allow you to jot down any ideas you have while the interview is going on.

6. *Thank the person you talked with.* After the interview, send a thank-you note. Remember that the person has shared valuable time with you.

7. *On your own or with a friend, go over what you learned in the interview.* Compare what you learned with your strengths and lifestyle choices. Decide if the match is good. If so, be happy. If not, be happy anyway. In either case, you've learned something important about yourself and your career.

8. *Do as many interviews as is necessary to get the information you want.* Remember, most people enjoy talking about their work. Most people also enjoy being helpful.

Someday you may be the one giving information in an interview. How important would a thank-you note be to you?

It's Worth Exploring

In coming chapters, you will read about careers in health care, sales, sports, and other areas. This book, however, can only begin to touch on these areas. It's up to you to explore careers in depth before you decide which one is right for you. Talk to counselors, read, and do informational interviews. The time and energy you spend can save you from jobs you won't like!

Chapter Review

Chapter Summary

- Talking to a career counselor, reading about a career, and doing informational interviews are three good ways to explore careers.

- Career centers and libraries have many helpful books for exploring careers. The *Guide to Occupational Exploration* (GOE) is useful for matching interests to careers. The *Dictionary of Occupational Titles* (DOT) lists over 20,000 jobs and briefly describes them. The *Occupational Outlook Handbook* includes the latest information about trends in over 250 careers. All three are good resources for finding possible careers and ruling out others.

- Informational interviews involve talking to people who have jobs that interest you. Informational interviews require preparation.

- Friends, family, teachers, career counselors, and professional associations are good ways to find people to interview.

- Steps in the informational interview include: 1. Finding the person who has the job or career you are interested in. 2. Making an appointment. 3. Preparing interview questions. 4. Keeping the appointment. 5. Keeping a record of the interview. 6. Sending a thank-you note. 7. Deciding if the career matches your strengths and lifestyle choices.

- Take the time now to explore careers. It can save you a lot of time and energy later. It can help you avoid jobs you wouldn't enjoy doing.

Chapter Quiz

Answer these questions on a separate sheet of paper.

A. Thinking About Careers

1. What does a photojournalist do?

2. How can a career counselor help you explore careers?

3. Name two places that have books used in exploring careers.

4. What is one career that a person with artistic interests might enjoy?

5. What career book matches 12 interest areas with possible careers?

6. In what book would you find a short job description of a roustabout?

7. In what book can you find the job outlook for a particular occupation?

8. What is an informational interview?

9. At what point in your job exploration should you do an informational interview?

10. What are two questions you might ask in an informational interview?

B. Putting What You Learned to Work

Look at your strengths and lifestyle choices. List one, two, or three careers that you may be interested in exploring. If you need ideas for careers, find the GOE, DOT, or OOH in a school or public library or in a career center. The librarian or career counselor can help you use it.

C. Work Out

Look up one of your career choices in the *Occupational Outlook Handbook*. (Again, your librarian or career counselor can help you with this task.) Does the job seem right for you? Why or why not? Describe how it matches or does not match your strengths and lifestyle choices.

Chapter 6

Careers in Health Care

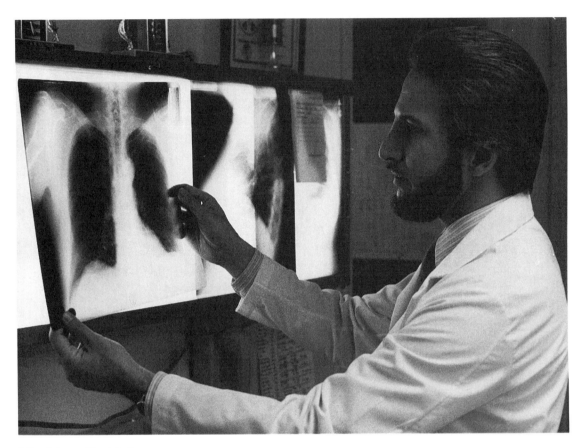

Machines that take x-rays are operated by x-ray technicians.

Chapter Learning Objectives

- Identify two health care fields.
- Describe two trends in health care.
- Match strengths and lifestyle choices to health care careers.
- List three ways to find out more about health care careers.

Words to Know

animal assistant   a person who assists veterinarians (animal doctors) in caring for animals

dental assistant   a person who assists dentists with patient care

dental hygienist   a person who cleans and takes x-rays of the teeth

health technician   a health worker who assists a health professional

home health care worker   a person who cares for a sick or disabled person in the home

licensed practical nurse (LPN)   a nurse who has completed a training program in patient care

mental health worker   a person who treats people suffering from mental or emotional problems

orderly   a hospital aid who helps care for patients

pharmacy assistant   a person who helps fill prescriptions

registered nurse (RN)   a nurse who has completed a two- or four-year program in patient care

veterinarian   an animal doctor

Bill stepped up to the plate. He held his bat high and waited for the pitch.

Thunk!

The next thing Bill knew, he was on the ground. The ball had connected with his head, not his bat. Instead of rounding the bases and heading for home, Bill was headed for the hospital.

The next few hours were full of medical tests. Finally, the doctor told Bill he could go home. He had to rest for several days and keep his head up.

On the way home in the car, Bill's mother warned him of the dangers of baseball.

"Oh, Mom," Bill said. "It's just a bump on the head."

"Well, I hope you learned something."

Bill rolled his eyes. "I did, Mom," he said. "I never realized all the different jobs there were in a hospital. First there was the nurse in the emergency room. Then an **orderly** wheeled me down the hall. An x-ray technician took an x-ray of my skull. On the way back to the waiting area, I saw the lab where blood is tested. There must have been ten people working in that place alone."

"What does that have to do with learning a lesson?" Bill's mother asked.

Bill answered. "I've always thought that having a career in health care meant being a doctor," Bill replied. "Doctors go to school for years. I didn't want to do that. Today I learned that there are many different careers in health care. I may end up working with a doctor, but I don't have to be one."

"In other words, young man," his mother said, "that ball knocked some sense into you."

Bill winced. "Aw, Mom," was all he could say.

Careers in Health Care

Like Bill, many of us think of doctors and nurses when we think about health care. But the number of health care fields is large, and there are many different types of health care jobs.

For example, some health care workers focus only on the teeth. A **dental hygienist** cleans a patient's teeth and takes x-rays. If there are problems, the dentist works to undo the harm that can be caused by sugar and junk food.

Mental health workers deal with the mind. They work with people who behave abnormally or who are simply dissatisfied with their lives. Mental illness can be caused by such things as a terrible event in a person's life, drug abuse, or a physical illness. Just as medical workers do, mental health workers try to prevent new problems as well as solve old ones. In the

Psychology is the study of the mind.

last 20 years, much has been written about how people can develop and maintain a healthy mental attitude.

Animal health is another health care field. Animal doctors are called **veterinarians.** They often have **animal assistants** to help them carry out their duties. Giving medicine, cleaning cages, and exercising animals are some of the things animal assistants do.

Job Trends in Health Care

The job outlook for careers in health care is good. In Chapter 2, you read that a large part of the population is growing older. As people age, they need more and more health care services. Also, health technology is changing quickly. Workers will be needed to operate the new equipment that is being created.

As a result, jobs in health care are growing at a faster than average rate. Employment in the health care industry rose from 7 million in 1988 to more than 9 million in July 1991. By 2005, the number of jobs is expected to grow to 12.8 million.

Nurses make up the largest group of workers in the health field.

Health care is also a changing industry. In the United States, health care is expensive. It is getting harder and harder for people to pay for treatment when they are sick. To solve this problem, the government is trying to find ways to make health care more efficient and to control costs.

This does not mean that there will be fewer jobs. It may affect the types of health care jobs available, however. For example, the number of careers in home health care is increasing. It has become very expensive to care for people in hospitals. It is less costly to care for people in their homes. **Home health care workers** give medications and help feed, dress, and comfort the ill and the disabled. In 1990, there were about 391,000 home health care workers in the United States.

More than five million people in the United States require home care services.

Careers Practice

1. What is the difference between a dental hygienist and a dentist?

2. What are two careers in the field of animal health?

3. What is one reason why the number of jobs in home health care services is increasing?

Are Your Strengths Right for a Health Care Career?

How can you decide if a career in health care is right for you? Think of your strengths and interests. Many people in health care have an interest in or aptitude for science. Do you like doing experiments? Have you done well in life science or health classes? If so, a career in health care might interest you.

Many careers in health care require a person who is kind and who cares about people. You must be a good listener. People should feel comfortable around you. Also, you must be willing and able to do unpleasant tasks, such as cleaning open wounds.

Health care workers should also be physically healthy and strong. Often, they have to move patients from one place to another. Mental health is also important. Many health care workers encounter sickness and death daily. They must be able to continue working yet not be unfeeling.

Most health care workers must be careful about details. For example, a **pharmacy assistant** helps fill prescriptions in drugstores. The assistant must be able to mix and measure medicines in exact amounts. A small slip could cause serious problems for a patient.

Some health care workers never come into contact with patients. For example, a dental technician works with tools in a lab to make false teeth.

Health Care and Lifestyle Choices

Careers in health care offer a wide range of lifestyle choices. Wherever there are people, health care is

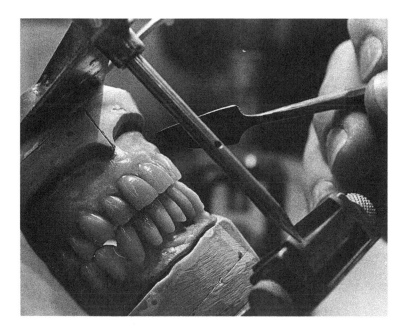

It takes skillful hands to make a set of false teeth.

needed. Opportunities are probably greater in cities and other highly populated areas. However, health care workers are often desperately needed in less-populated areas as well.

Health care jobs are found in many different environments. Hospitals are the largest employer of health care workers. Because they operate day and night, hospitals need workers on afternoon, evening, and night shifts, as well as daytime hours. Weekend workers are also needed.

Clinics and doctors' offices also employ health care workers. A doctor's office is much smaller than a hospital. Most offices are open only during the day, and they might be closed on weekends. Working in a doctor's office gives some workers the chance to specialize. Quite often, a doctor will only treat certain types of illnesses.

As you read earlier, health care is also done in the patient's home. Because they work one-on-one, home health care workers often develop close relationships with their patients. They also work different shifts, especially when around-the-clock care is needed.

Education, training, and income vary widely in the health care field. Usually, the more education and training you have, the greater your income. Colleges, community colleges, and vocational schools offer training for numerous health care careers. These training programs can last several months to several years. Some hospitals train people for entry-level jobs as well.

In Texas and California, licensed practical nurses are called licensed vocational nurses, or LVNs.

Close Up: Career Ladder in Nursing

Lyle has been a nurse for 15 years. Here is how he went up the career ladder to earn more money.

When Lyle graduated from high school, he took a job as a nurse's aid in a home for elderly people. He received on-the-job training under a trained nurse. Lyle helped dress and feed people. He earned the minimum wage. (Today, a nursing home nurse's aid's salary ranges from about $8,300 to $11,000 per year.)

After three years, Lyle went into a training program to become a **licensed practical nurse (LPN).** He took classes at a local community college. Then he took a test required by the state to become licensed. At the nursing home, Lyle's pay and job duties both increased. (Today, LPNs' average salaries range from $13,000 to $18,000 per year.)

Lyle continued to take courses. Finally, he completed a four-year program and became a **registered nurse (RN).** As an RN, Lyle could supervise other nurses. He left the nursing home and took a job at a hospital. He now earns $30,000 per year.

Careers Practice

1. What "people skills" do most health care workers need?

2. If you were a nurse and wanted to work a night shift, where might you apply?

3. What is an LPN?

How to Learn More About Careers in Health Care

Does a career in health care sound right for you? If so, you might want to research health care jobs a bit more. Here are some ideas:

1. Read through job descriptions of health careers in the *Occupational Outlook Handbook* (OOH) or in other resources. Health careers may fall into many different categories, so look carefully. For example, doctors, nurses, and veterinarians are found in the professional group. An x-ray technician falls in the **health technicians** category. Health technicians assist health professionals. Other health workers, such as **dental assistants,** are classified under service occupations.

2. Do further research on any of these careers in your school or public library or career center.

3. Speak with anyone you know who has experience in or knowledge of health careers.

4. Do informational interviews.

5. Volunteer in a nursing home or hospital. You may not get to work directly with patients. You will, however, get an idea of what it's like to work in these settings. Also, you will be around many health professionals. You may find a good person to interview.

Nursing homes and hospitals often welcome volunteers.

6. Contact your local vocational school or community college. Ask them to send you information on any health career training programs they have. Whenever possible, ask about a specific career. Otherwise, you may be sent more information than you want.

7. Take science and health classes. If your school offers a psychology class, take it.

8. Write to professional associations for information. Some key associations are listed below.

When you write, be clear about what you want to know. For example, John wanted to know about careers in animal health. Here is a letter he wrote. He included information about his interests and where he wants to live. This could make it easier for the person receiving the letter to send John just what he wants.

United States Animal Health
  Association
P.O. Box 28176
6924 Lakeside Avenue, Suite 205
Richmond, VA 23228

Dear USAHA,

I am a high school student with a great love for animals, especially horses. I think I would greatly enjoy a career working with animals. I am writing to you for career information.

I am an average science student and a good, strong worker. I am not interested in going to college for four years. However, I would be willing to take some classes if it would help me prepare for a career.

Can you suggest any fields in animal health that might be good to pursue? Also, any information on training programs in my area would be helpful. I would like to work in Ohio, if possible.

Thank you for your help.

Sincerely,

John Sherman

John Sherman

Health Care Associations

American Medical Association
535 North Dearborn Street
Chicago, IL 60610

American Nurses Association
2420 Pershing Road
Kansas City, MO 64108

American Dental Association
211 East Chicago Avenue
Chicago, IL 60611

American Health Care Association
1201 L Street NW
Washington, DC 20005

United States Animal Health Association
P.O. Box 28176
6924 Lakeside Avenue, Suite 205
Richmond, VA 23228

National Mental Health Association
1021 Prince Street
Alexandria, VA 22314-2971

Chapter Review

Chapter Summary

- There are many health care fields and many health care careers. Some people work to prevent and cure physical illnesses. Others work in the field of mental health. They specialize in the human mind. Some health care workers choose to work only with animals. There are careers for just about every interest.

- Jobs in health care are increasing. This is partly due to the aging population. Changing technology is also creating jobs.

- Home health care workers take care of the ill and the disabled in their homes. There may be a need for many more home health care workers in the future.

- It is helpful for a health care worker to be interested in science. He or she should also like working with people. Health care workers must pay attention to detail. Many health care workers face sickness and death every day on the job. They should be healthy themselves.

- There are health care careers to fit just about any lifestyle. Cities offer the most job opportunities. However, health care is needed everywhere. Shifts are available days, nights, overnight, and on weekends. As a rule, income increases with training and education.

- Health care career training programs can be found in colleges, community colleges, and vocational schools. Hospitals sometimes offer on-the-job training for entry-level positions.

- To find out more about health care, take classes in life sciences, health, and psychology. Talk to health care workers. Volunteer in a nursing home or a hospital. Do research in a library or career center. Write to colleges and professional associations.

Chapter Quiz

Answer these questions on a separate sheet of paper.

A. Thinking About Careers

1. What are two careers in the field of dental health?

2. What do people in the field of mental health specialize in?

3. How many health care jobs were there in 1991?

4. How many health care jobs are there expected to be in 2005?

5. Why must a pharmacy assistant pay attention to details?

6. Why are there more health care job opportunities in the city than in the country?

7. Name four places where one might be able to train for the health care field.

8. Who will probably have a higher income, an LPN or an RN? Why?

9. What is a health technician?

10. Where might a person do volunteer work if he or she is interested in a health care career?

B. Putting What You Learned to Work

Are your strengths and lifestyle choices suitable to a career in health care? Write a short explanation of why they are or are not. If you are interested in a health care career, which field interests you the most?

C. Work Out

Optometrists are vision care specialists. They help improve people's eyesight by fitting them with glasses. They do not perform surgery or prescribe drugs. Helping the optometrist is the optometric technician. This person might give vision tests and help fit glasses What strengths do you think an optometric technician needs?

Chapter 7

Careers in Sales

Working in a retail store is a good way to learn sales skills.

Chapter Learning Objectives

- Identify two types of sales careers.
- Describe trends in sales careers.
- Match strengths and lifestyle choices to sales careers.
- List three ways to find out more about sales careers.

Words to Know

bonus something given in addition to what is usual or expected

commission a fee paid to a sales worker for selling goods or services, usually a percentage of the sale price

consumer a person who buys goods or services

direct sale the sale of goods or services directly to a consumer, not through a store

minimum wage the lowest hourly amount of money that a business can legally pay its workers

negotiate to bargain

persistence continuing on a course of action even when difficulties arise

persuade to make someone willing to do or believe something

real estate property

retail having to do with selling directly to the public

telemarketing the selling of products and services over the telephone

---

Mr. Solomon's civics class had taken on a worthy project. The students' goal was to raise $5,000 for a local homeless shelter. To raise the money, they decided to have a dance. Tickets to the dance would cost $25 each. The class would have to sell 200 tickets.

Roxy and Lou worked on the dance committee. They **persuaded** restaurant owners to donate the food. A party store provided decorations. A hotel agreed to hold the dance in one of its ballrooms. Roxy managed to get a band to play at the dance for free.

Lisa and her friends handled the ads. They made posters and put them up all around the city. They wrote an article in the school paper about the fundraising event. Lisa also got a reporter to write about the upcoming dance in the city newspaper.

Jill, Tom, and Phil took charge of ticket sales. They sold them door-to-door. At sporting events, they set up a ticket booth. Phil even gave out his phone number so that people could call in orders. (For once, his father didn't mind that Phil was always on the phone.)

The dance was a big success. Mr. Solomon's class sold more than 300 tickets. The homeless shelter received over $7,500!

Later, Mr. Solomon praised his students. "You were wonderful," he smiled. "You're the best group of salespeople I've ever seen."

Careers in Sales

Mr. Solomon's students had not thought of themselves as sales workers. They were, however, doing what most sales workers do. They were persuading others to buy—or donate—goods or services.

Sales workers are the link between businesses and **consumers.** Businesses produce goods and services. Consumers buy those goods and services. Sales workers show us products, give us information, take our money, and arrange for deliveries. Without sales workers, it would be harder to buy a new car or even just a bag of apples.

There are as many sales jobs as there are goods and services. The largest number of sales careers are in the **retail** sales area. Retail sales workers are employed by stores to help customers find what they need. They ring up the sales at cash registers. Retail sales workers sell food, clothing, TVs, CDs, plants, computers, pet food, and more. Usually, the amount of goods sold to each customer is fairly small.

Service sales workers sell services rather than goods. For example, banks have service workers who help customers sign up for checking accounts and other banking services. Telephone companies employ sales workers to sell consumers their long distance services. Newspapers employ service sales workers to sell advertising space. Travel agents sell trips and tours. The list could go on and on.

People also find careers as manufacturers' sales workers. These people work for companies that produce goods. Their job is to sell the product to retail

Sales workers are often called sales or marketing *representatives*.

Some people make a living selling things to others in their homes.

stores and other businesses. For example, Jerry is a manufacturer's sales worker for the Dandy Paint Company. He contacts paint and hardware stores in the northern part of his state. He tries to persuade the store owners to carry Dandy Paint. When he gets an order, he bills the store and sees that the paint is delivered on time. He also follows up on the sale to make sure the store owner is happy.

Some sales workers handle **direct sales.** The direct sales worker gets a product and sells it to the consumer. No store is involved. For instance, many people are familiar with Avon and Mary Kay cosmetics. These companies employ direct sales workers. The sales workers might go door-to-door or invite customers into their homes to try out the products. Toys, magazines, and kitchenware are some other items sold though direct sales.

Job Trends in Sales

If you are interested in a sales career, the overall job outlook is good. The Bureau of Labor Statistics believes that the number of sales jobs will increase 24 percent by the year 2005. About 17 million Americans will have jobs in sales then. The service sales field is growing at a faster rate than other sales fields. For example, there are a growing number of jobs for people who sell insurance.

Thanks to technology, sales can be done faster and better than ever before. For example, retail sales workers used to have to carefully enter prices into their cash registers. Then they would figure out a customer's change in their heads. Today's cash registers are much "smarter." In many stores, the sales worker simply slides a sensing device across a bar code on a price tag. The cash register "reads" each code and adds up prices. It also figures the tax and the correct change due the customer.

Because of technology, some sales jobs are disappearing. Vending machines have replaced snack bars in many companies, for example. Some kinds of shopping can be done by personal computer without the need for a salesperson. Cashiers may be gone from the grocery stores of the future. Such stores will become "self-serve," as many gas stations already are today.

At the same time, technology is creating new types of sales jobs. **Telemarketing** is a new field in which all sales are done by phone. And for each new, improved product, there must be someone to sell it. It is unlikely that sales careers will ever disappear entirely.

Careers Practice

1. If you sell magazines door-to-door, are you in direct sales or retail sales?

2. Suppose you work for a company that produces soap. You sell the soap to stores. They, in turn, sell the soap to customers. Are you a services sales worker or a manufacturer's sales worker?

3. Are sales jobs expected to increase in the United States?

Are Your Strengths Right for a Sales Career?

In every sales job, you must have a good knowledge of what you are selling. However, knowing a lot about cars won't make you a good car salesperson. You might be better driving or fixing them!

As a consumer, what qualities do you like in a salesperson?

Good sales workers know how to persuade people. They must be able to convince customers that their products are the best available. This can be done by comparing products, giving demonstrations, and listing facts. Most consumers want to trust the sales workers they buy from. Friendliness, honesty, charm, and **persistence** all work in salespeople's favor.

Want ads for sales workers often ask for "self-starters." Self-starters go out and get customers—they don't wait for customers to come to them. Self-starters take risks by calling on possible customers who may or may not want to be bothered. They also use ads, sales, and special discounts to get new business. They are always thinking of new ways to make sales.

Sales people should also have math skills. They add up prices, and in some cases **negotiate** discounts. They should be able to keep good, clear records. Sales workers often keep files on customers and what they have bought. They may use these files to stay in touch with customers and make future sales.

Sales Careers and Lifestyle Choices

Where and how you live depends very much on the type of sales job you have. Retail sales workers usually live near the stores that employ them. Manufacturers' sales workers usually live near the companies they work for, but they might often travel. People involved in direct sales might work only in nearby neighborhoods. Some telemarketers work entirely at home. They can live and work wherever there are phone lines.

What would you like or not like about working at home?

The amount of time a person spends doing sales work can also vary greatly. Right now, one quarter of all sales jobs are held by part-time employees who work less than 35 hours per week. Some sales jobs are quite a bit more demanding. They may require long hours and many trips away from home.

What kind of education and training does it take to get a sales job? Quite often, retail sales jobs are held by people with high school diplomas. Some companies provide training programs to teach people about products or to sharpen their sales skills. Some sales jobs require people to pass state exams and get licenses. People who sell **real estate,** for example, must be licensed.

Higher education can also be quite helpful to people who want sales careers. Both two- and four-year colleges offer courses and degrees in advertising, marketing, and business. More than 25 percent of salespeople have college degrees.

What kind of income can you expect as a sales-person? Retail sales workers usually earn hourly wages. Quite often, they start at **minimum wage** and get small raises over time. In order to earn more, they must become supervisors or managers.

Some salespeople work only on **commission.** This means the worker gets a certain percentage of each sale. For example, Mr. Smith, a real estate agent, sells a house for $100,000. He gets six percent of the sale, or $6,000. Working on commission may sound great. However, it is only for people who are patient and who like working under pressure. It may take months or years to make a big sale. And there is never any guarantee that the sale will be made.

Sales people sometimes earn small base salaries along with their commissions and bonuses. A **bonus** is an amount of money awarded to a person who sells a certain amount and does an outstanding job. For example, a company could award a bonus of $500 to its top sales worker each month.

Careers Practice

Answer these questions on a separate sheet of paper.

1. Explain how you can have a sales job but never see customers.

2. What does it mean to work on commission?

3. What is the typical income for a new retail sales worker?

Close Up: Career Ladder in Sales

Fran was a born salesperson. She loved to talk and to persuade people to see things her way. People liked her, and she liked them.

When Fran was still in high school, she applied for a job in retail sales. She was given a part-time job in the candy department of a large store. Soon Fran learned all about chocolates. She taught some of her best customers to tell the difference between Swiss and American chocolate. As you can imagine, she was quite popular.

The manager of the candy department saw Fran's strengths. When Fran finished high school, she asked Fran to work full-time. She put Fran through extra sales training. She also started to give her bonuses when she sold a lot of candy.

After several years, Fran became bored with candy. She wanted to earn more money and have bigger challenges. She found that her sales skills could be used in many different settings. Fran became the manager of an electronics store. Now she trains other people to sell TVs and CD players. Quite often, she rewards her salespeople with boxes of the finest chocolate money can buy!

How to Learn More About Careers in Sales

By now, you may have formed an idea of whether or not a sales career would be right for you. If you think it is, do some research. Look in printed resources at the many different types of sales jobs there are. Interview a salesperson. Good ones like to talk. You should be able to find someone who is willing to share his or her experiences with you.

Here are six other ways to learn more about sales work. These activities will also sharpen your sales skills.

1. *Get a temporary job in sales.* Quite often, large department stores need extra help at holiday time. They are good places to apply for your first sales job. If possible, sell items you're interested in or know something about. You will learn basic

By taking part in debates, students learn to persuade.

customer service skills. As you work, watch how experienced people do their jobs.

2. *Join a debate team.* Debaters choose a subject and then argue one side or the other. They learn to persuade with the facts and with enthusiasm and other emotions. In many ways, debaters are learning sales skills that they can use on many jobs.

3. *Become a fundraising volunteer for a cause you believe in.* You can work for a political campaign, a charity, or an environmental group. Getting donations is one of the toughest sales jobs there is. It is a great way to practice and learn sales skills.

4. *Read and listen carefully to ads.* Ads persuade just as sales workers do. Decide which ads are the most effective.

5. *Take classes in business math, sales, or advertising at your high school or community college.* You don't need to have a college degree to get into a sales career. However, you do want to have good sales skills. Taking such classes will help you reach that goal.

6. *Write to one or more of the sales associations listed below.*

Sales Associations

National Association for Professional Saleswomen
P.O. Box 2606
Novato, CA 94948

Professional Salespersons of America
3801 Monaco, NE
Albuquerque, NM 87211

Direct Selling Association
1776 K Street, NW, Suite 600
Washington, DC 20006

National Retail Merchants Association
100 West 31st Street
New York, NY 10001

Chapter Review

Chapter Summary

- Sales workers link consumers with businesses. They show products, make sales, and arrange deliveries.

- Retail sales workers are employed by stores. They sell goods to consumers. Service sales workers sell services. Manufacturers' sales workers are employed by companies that produce goods that are sold to stores or other businesses. People who handle direct sales bypass stores and sell directly to consumers.

- Technology is helping sales people do their jobs faster and more accurately. It is both eliminating jobs and creating new sales jobs. Sales jobs are expected to increase 24 percent by the year 2005. At that time, about 17 million people will work in sales.

- Friendliness, honesty, charm, and persistence are good traits for a sales person to have. Many sales positions require a person who is a self-starter. Math and record keeping skills are important strengths.

- Some sales jobs require travel, while others are done at home or in stores. There are part-time and full-time opportunities. Sales training can be found in companies and in two-year and four-year colleges. Some sales jobs require licenses.

- Sales workers often receive hourly wages. They may also work on commission or for bonuses.

- To learn more about sales, you can get a temporary sales job; join a debate team; study ads; do fund-raising; or take sales classes. Of course you can also do research in a library or career center, speak with people who have already done this work, and write to sales associations.

Chapter Quiz

Answer these questions on a separate sheet of paper.

A. Thinking About Careers

1. What machine do many retail sales workers operate?

2. What are two things a service sales representative might sell?

3. John works for a company that produces furniture. He sells the furniture to department stores. They, in turn, sell it to consumers. What type of sales job does John have?

4. How might technology affect future sales jobs in grocery stores?

5. What are two strengths of a good salesperson?

6. Could you have a career in sales and work at home? Explain.

7. John earns 10 percent of the price on every item he sells. What is this an example of?

8. What is a bonus?

9. How are salespeople and debate team members alike?

10. What is a good place to get a first sales job?

B. Putting What You Learned to Work

Are your strengths and lifestyle choices suitable to a career in sales? Write a short explanation of why they are or are not. If you are interested in a sales career, which products or services would you like to sell? Why?

C. Work Out

Write a story about Sarah. She goes door-to-door selling *Weight Away*, a magazine about losing weight. What does she say when a customer opens the door? How does she try to persuade a customer who shows little interest in what she is selling?

Chapter 8
Careers in Technology

Technicians help plan, install, run, and repair equipment and machines.

Chapter Learning Objectives

- Identify two kinds of careers in technology.
- Describe trends in technology-related careers.
- Match strengths and lifestyle choices to careers in technology.
- List three ways to find out more about careers in technology.

Words to Know

automotive technician a person who builds, maintains, and repairs cars

broadcast technician a person who installs, runs, and repairs equipment used by TV and radio stations

computer service technician a person who installs, maintains, and repairs computers

diving technician a person who works on underwater projects

drafting technician a person who helps draw the plans for such things as buildings and machines

fire safety technician a person who inspects buildings for fire safety

heating and air conditioning technician a person who builds, maintains, and repairs heating and air conditioning equipment

mechanical technician a person who installs, maintains, and repairs machines in plants or factories

plastics technician a person who helps develop and test plastic materials

robotics technician a person who installs, maintains, and repairs robots

---

Paula and Guy sat on the beach. Tomorrow would be the first day of their last year of high school.

"What do you want to do after you leave school?" Paula asked playfully.

"Promise you won't laugh?" Guy replied.

"I promise."

Guy pointed to the ocean. "I want to hunt for buried treasure," he said. "I got the idea from a story I read. In 1622, the *Santa Margarita,* a Spanish ship, sank off the coast of Florida. Supposedly she was filled with treasure. In 1980, a crew of divers using modern equipment found her. Do you know what they brought up? Over 20 million dollars' worth of treasure!"

Paula stared out at the sea. "Wow! 'Guy Smith, Treasure Diver.' I like the sound of that."

Guy took Paula's hand and smiled.

Careers in Technology

Why might oil companies employ diving technicians?

Career counselors have a less romantic name than "treasure diver" for Guy's dream career. People who work on underwater projects are called **diving technicians**. Most diving technicians make their living by helping build underwater structures.

Technicians are important people in today's fast-paced world. They help carry out the plans of scientists, engineers, and other professionals. Most technicians set up, run, program, and repair electronic equipment and machines. Without them, cable TV, computers, and the space shuttle would still be only ideas.

Health technicians are often placed in the technical careers category. See Chapter 6 in this book for information about health technicians.

Quite often, when people think of technical careers they think of computers. Thanks to computers, many new technical jobs have been created, and the number of jobs is increasing all the time. **Computer service technicians**, for example, rank fifth on the Department of Labor's "top ten list" of fastest-growing jobs. These technicians install, maintain, and repair computer systems.

Technical jobs are also available in the building industry. For example, **drafting technicians** draw detailed plans for building projects. They work with engineers and architects to design safe, strong, workable buildings. **Heating and air conditioning technicians** specialize in keeping buildings at the proper temperatures.

Manufacturing companies also employ technicians. A **mechanical technician** could install and repair large and small machines in a factory. A team of **automotive technicians** might help a car designer put together the car of the future. A **plastics technician** might work in a laboratory to help a chemist design stronger materials.

Technicians also find employment in the broadcasting industry. In general, **broadcast**

technicians install and operate radio and TV equipment. Technicians are also used to make movies and to put on plays and rock concerts.

Ten Fastest-Growing Occupations through the Year 2000

1. Paralegal
2. Medical assistant
3. Physical therapist
4. Physical and corrective therapy assistant
5. Computer service technician
6. Home health aid
7. Podiatrist
8. Computer systems analyst
9. Medical records technician
10. Employment interviewer

Source: *Department of Labor Statistics*, 1987

Job Trends in Technology

The number of jobs in technical areas is not as great as in areas such as office jobs or sales. However, the number of jobs in the technical group is expected to increase 37 percent by the year 2005. (Health technologists account for more than half of the 4.5 million jobs in this group.)

What does the growth rate mean in terms of opportunities? Because many technical fields are quite new, opportunities might be limited now. However, the future looks bright. The field of robotics is a good example. Right now, about 30,000 robots are being used in U.S. plants. In ten years, however, experts predict that 250,000 more robots will take the place of four million workers. Fortunately, companies will need **robotics technicians** to install, care for, and repair

Job growth in broadcasting is much slower than in other technical fields.

the robots. Technology will take away assembly-line jobs and replace some of them with jobs for technicians.

Careers Practice

Answer these questions on a separate sheet of paper.

1. Who could a drafting technician work for?

2. Are most technical jobs growing at a fast rate or a slow rate?

3. What does a robotics technician do?

Are Your Strengths Right for a Career in Technology?

Suppose that one stormy night the lights in your house suddenly go out. Do you light a candle and wait for them to come back on? Or do you try to figure out how to solve the problem?

If you chose "light a candle and wait," you might *not* want to consider a technical career. Technical people are problem solvers who like working with *things*— perhaps more than with people. They are at home with the inner workings of computers and TVs. They like to know how things work and how to fix them.

In general, technical people need good mechanical skills. They often use hand tools (drills, screwdrivers, and so on) in their work. They must be able to understand and apply mechanical principles. Remember Guy at the beginning of this chapter? He wanted to become a diving technician and recover sunken treasure. However, just knowing how to dive wouldn't be enough. Guy would have to know how to hook up underwater pulleys in just the right way. He'd need to consider ocean currents, the weight of the ship, and other matters.

Technical workers often have to follow detailed written instructions. To do so, they must be good readers. Good math skills are also a must for the technicians of the future. Many technical training programs require students to take algebra and trigonometry. These are tough subjects, but they're a must for those who'll be working in science and engineering.

The best technicians are team players who can take directions well and play their parts. Good communication skills are important, too. Technicians don't have to love to talk in the way that salespeople sometimes do. They simply must be able to talk clearly about a project and what needs to be done to complete it.

Would you be comfortable wearing a tool belt to work every day?

Technical Careers and Lifestyle Choices

Technicians' jobs can be found in many different settings. Technicians work for power companies, building firms, banks, TV stations, and more.

Most technicians work daytime shifts. Many jobs are inside office buildings or in factory-like settings. However, there are always exceptions. A broadcast technician might work all night to help TV reporters film a story. A diving technician's office is aboard ship. An automotive technician could spend time at a race track studying how a car performs. The work environment differs with the nature and duty of the job.

To be a technician, a person must be prepared to make a commitment to education. Very few technician jobs go to young people just out of high school. At least two years of training in a special field is required. Training programs may allow a person to work part-time while going to school. However, they also demand study time and hard work. Even after being hired, a technician must be prepared to keep up on the latest advances in his or her field. For technicians, training is a lifelong activity.

Does the schooling pay off? In most cases, yes. Technicians generally will get starting jobs with salaries ranging from $15,000 to $20,000 per year. However, with time and experience, good technicians in most fields will earn over $30,000.

Fire fighters must have good technical skills.

Careers Practice

Answer these questions on a separate sheet of paper.

1. Do technicians prefer to work with things or with people?

2. Why do technicians have to be good readers?

3. What is the least amount of training that most high school graduates need to become technicians?

Technical Careers in the Fire Department

Jill had always wanted to be a fire fighter. She thought a fire fighter's career demanded only strength and courage. When she passed the entrance exam and started training, however, Jill began to think differently. She found that fire fighters must have technical skills as well.

Jill had to learn how to operate, clean, and repair fire-fighting equipment. Her teachers explained how fires spread through buildings and landscapes. Fire fighters have to be aware of these principles to decide how best to fight fires. Fighting fires requires careful, practical thinking.

Jill was good at the technical part of her job. Eventually, she became a **fire safety technician**. Now she has other duties besides fighting fires. She inspects buildings for fire safety. She also makes recommendations on how to correct problems in buildings. Jill considers herself part engineer, part builder, and part fire fighter.

How to Learn More About Careers in Technology

Technical jobs are often billed as "the jobs of the future." To get such a job, you must be willing to invest time and money in school. When you look up technical job descriptions, look carefully at job opportunities and income. If technical jobs still interest you, locate a person who is willing to be interviewed. You can also do one or all of the following activities to develop your technical interests and skills.

1. Work on the lighting or sound crews for your school play. You will use technical equipment, follow directions, and work as part of a team.

2. Develop your math skills. Begin with algebra. If you do well, try trigonometry. You do not have to be an "A" student. However, you should get better than average grades if you're thinking about working in the engineering field.

What technical classes or activities does your school offer?

3. Some high schools offer classes in drafting and auto repair. Take one or both to test your interests.

4. Flip through the yellow pages of your phone book. Make a list of the types and numbers of businesses that could hire technicians. For starters, look under *Computers, Builders,* and *Electric.*

5. Build scale models of airplanes, cars, buildings— whatever interests you. You'll learn a lot about how things are put together. You'll also get a better idea of your technical skills.

6. Write to one of the following associations for more information.

Technology-Related Career Associations

Educational and Training Division
Robotics International
American Society of Manufacturing Engineers
P.O. Box 930
Dearborn, MI 48128

National Action Council for Minorities in
  Engineering
3 West 35th Street
New York, NY 10001

Junior Engineering Technical Society
  (JETS)
1428 King Street, Suite 405
Alexandria, VA 22314

Society of Broadcast Engineers
Information Office
7002 Graham Road, Suite 118
Indianapolis, IN 46220

Chapter Review

Chapter Summary

- Technicians are important people in today's fast-paced world. They help carry out the plans of scientists, engineers, and other professionals. Most technicians set up, run, program, and repair electronic equipment and machines.

- Technicians work in a variety of fields. For example, they assist professionals in the building industry, in manufacturing, and in broadcasting.

- The number of jobs for technicians is growing quickly. Opportunities in some fields are limited now but should improve.

- Technicians must have mechanical skills and like to solve problems. They often prefer to work with things rather than people. However, they must still be able to communicate clearly about projects and work as part of a team. Good reading and math skills are a must.

- Most technician jobs are in office or factory settings. Would-be technicians must make a commitment to attend school for at least two years after high school. To keep up with advances, technicians must continue to learn throughout their careers.

- To test and develop your technical interests, work on the lighting or sound crew for a school play. Take classes in algebra, auto shop, and drafting. Identify local businesses who use technicians. Build scale models. Be sure of your interests before committing yourself to a technical career.

Chapter Quiz

Answer the following questions on a separate sheet of paper.

A. Thinking About Careers

1. What does a computer service technician do?

2. What does an automotive technician do?

3. List two technical jobs in the building industry.

4. At what rate is the number of technical jobs increasing?

5. How are robots creating new jobs?

6. Who needs to be more persuasive, a computer salesperson or a computer service technician?

7. Who is more likely to be mechanically minded, a home health aid or an auto technician?

8. Do most technicians work as part of a team?

9. What do most high school graduates have to do to get work as technicians?

10. Bill is working as a lighting technician for the school play. What skills is he developing?

B. Putting What You Learned to Work

Are your strengths and lifestyle choices suitable to a career as a technician? Tell why or why not.

C. Work Out

Choose one of the technical jobs mentioned in this chapter. Imagine that you have trained for it. Do you think you will have a hard time or an easy time finding work in your town? Tell why.

Chapter 9

Careers in the Office

Office careers require people who can juggle many tasks at once.

Chapter Learning Objectives

- Identify two kinds of office careers.
- Describe trends in office careers.
- Match strengths and lifestyle choices to office careers.
- List three ways to find out more about office careers.

Words to Know

accounts receivable clerk a person who keeps records of incoming money

billing clerk a person who records and sends out bills

bookkeeper a person who keeps records on business expenses and income

clerical relating to clerks or office workers

clerical supervisor a person who trains and oversees clerks

file clerk a person who organizes paperwork and puts it into files

payroll clerk a person who makes sure that paychecks are correct and that they're delivered on time

receptionist a person who receives customers or guests in an office or hotel

secretary a person who answers phones, types letters, and performs other duties in an office

shipping and receiving clerk a person in a stock room or warehouse who is involved with receiving incoming goods and shipping outgoing goods

stock clerk a persons who shelves and packages goods in a stock room or warehouse

ticket agent a person who provides facts about travel schedules, makes customer reservations, and sells tickets

word processor a person who enters letters and other written documents into a computer

Linda wanted to get good job skills. To do so, she joined the volunteer work program at her high school. Her counselor placed her in the school office. For an hour a day, Linda would act as the **receptionist**. She would answer phone calls and greet visitors to the office.

On her first day, the office supervisor showed Linda how to answer the phones and transfer calls. She also showed her how to take messages.

"This will be a snap," Linda thought to herself. "What's the big deal about working in an office?"

On her second day, Linda found out. At 8:00 A.M., all three phone lines started ringing at once. Linda tried to forward calls and put people on hold. Several times, however, she hung up on people instead. An angry parent called back.

"Why did you hang up on me?" the parent screamed. "I pay my taxes. I deserve better treatment than that."

Meanwhile, a line of students had formed at the counter. The boy at the front of the line began drumming his fingers on the countertop. "Hey, can I get some help here?" he asked. "I'm going to be late for class."

Just then, Mr. Plum, the principal, came out of his office. "Linda, have you made the coffee yet? Our last volunteer worker always made coffee first thing in the morning."

If you were Linda, how would you have handled things?

When her hour was up, Linda left the office with her head spinning. "Talking on the phone is easy," she later told her friends. "It's juggling different tasks at once that I've got to learn!"

Careers in the Office

Linda found out that office workers have the very important role of helping an office run smoothly. They handle mail, phone calls, paperwork, and more.

Office workers are sometimes called **clerical** workers. There are many clerical jobs. However, most of them can be put into several large groups.

Information clerks are responsible for greeting and assisting customers or visitors. Receptionists, hotel clerks, and **ticket agents** are all examples of information clerks. Workers with these jobs often perform other duties, such as taking messages, assigning hotel rooms, or issuing tickets. However, their main job is to inform people about the services their businesses offer.

Record clerks keep track of paperwork. Quite often, the paperwork is related to money. **Billing clerks** send out bills. **Accounts receivable clerks** keep track of what bills have or have not been paid. **Bookkeepers** record expenses and income. **Payroll clerks** keep records on employee hours and figure out paychecks. **File clerks** spend the main part of their days putting paperwork where it belongs.

Another group of clerical workers is in charge of shipping and receiving. **Stock clerks** keep track of the goods in stock rooms and warehouses. They record which items are entering and leaving. They unpack incoming goods and store them. If they work for retail stores, they may put the goods out on the sales floor.

Shipping and receiving clerks do similar work. They, too, are involved in keeping track of goods. However, they are more concerned with receiving goods and shipping them out than stock clerks are. They see that orders for goods are correctly filled and that goods are packaged properly.

Secretaries are also clerical workers. They typically have a wide range of job duties. Usually, they are assigned to one or more people in a company. The secretary answers phones, types letters, runs errands, and so on. **Word processors** specialize in entering business letters and other written documents into computers. **Clerical supervisors** and managers train and oversee other office workers.

There are dozens of other jobs in the clerical field.

Job Trends in Office Careers

About 20 million workers are employed in clerical jobs. More Americans have jobs in this category than in any other. The number of clerical jobs is expected to grow about 13 percent by the year 2005. Many of the new jobs will be for information clerks. There may, however, be a decrease in certain jobs, such as word

Which job appeals to you more, billing clerk or receptionist?

processors, bookkeepers, and telephone operators. Can you guess why?

How might answering machines affect the need for office workers?

Technology is the reason. Computers, copiers, and other office machines enable office workers to produce more at faster rates. As a result, fewer office workers may be needed to run offices. Copy machines, for example, can copy, sort, and even staple papers.

Careers Practice

Answer these questions on a separate sheet of paper.

1. What is another name for office workers?

2. What do stock clerks do?

3. Is the number of jobs for word processors expected to increase or decrease?

Are Your Strengths Right for an Office Career?

Do you always hang up your coat? Is your locker neat and tidy? Do you like to brush your teeth at the same time every day?

If an employer looked in your closet right now, would he or she be impressed with your neatness?

If so, an office career may be right for you. Office workers, no matter what their duties are, should be careful, accurate, and well organized. A file clerk who misplaces important papers will not last long with a company. Nor will a payroll clerk who forgets to deliver the checks on Friday!

For the most part, clerical jobs are very routine. Stock clerks, for example, perform pretty much the same duties day after day. Some jobs require a worker to be more flexible. A clerical supervisor could have to figure out how to reassign work when two clerks are out with the flu. A receptionist might have to handle

Warehouse workers sometimes operate forklifts.

20 callers in 10 minutes. In such cases, knowing which demands to respond to first is important. So is staying calm.

As a rule, office workers must have some mechanical or technical skills as well. A typical office could have several computers, a copy machine, and a typewriter. Warehouse workers could have to weigh goods on an electronic scale or run a forklift. (This is a large machine that is used to lift and stack heavy objects. It is often mounted on a small truck.) Being willing and able to operate these machines is a big part of the office worker's job.

Office Careers and Lifestyle Choices

Office workers are needed in just about every type of business. Banks need bank tellers. Health clubs need receptionists. Bookstores need stock clerks. Even your school employs office workers.

Most office positions are daytime jobs. The usual working hours are between 8 A.M. and 5 P.M. Most offices are closed on weekends. Workers in stock rooms might have afternoon or midnight shifts. Some ticket agents, such as those employed by airlines, might have to work any shift.

A clerk could work in an office or a warehouse. Most offices are clean, well-lighted places that are pleasant to work in. Workers dress neatly and professionally. In warehouses, workers may face damp or cold conditions. More likely than not, they will dress in clothing that allows them to do physical work comfortably.

Does your school offer any business skills classes? If so, what are they?

Most beginning clerical jobs require high school diplomas. Students could take classes in business math, office machines, or bookkeeping to better their chances of being hired. Some businesses offer on-the-job training to help workers sharpen their skills and advance.

How much can you expect to earn as an office worker? A stock clerk usually starts at about $4.25 an hour. However, with experience, that worker might earn as much as $10 an hour. Bookkeepers earn between $14,000 and $20,000 per year. Secretaries' incomes range from $16,000 to $28,000. Clerical supervisors and managers use more skills and have more responsibilities than most other office workers. With experience, they might earn over $30,000. Basically, the more skills and experience you have, the more you will earn.

Careers Practice

Answer these questions on a separate sheet of paper.

1. Should a person considering an office job like routine? Why?

2. What are three typical duties of a secretary?

3. What classes could you take to prepare for an office career?

Banks employ clerical workers.

Close Up: Career Ladder in the Bank

In high school, Peter took classes in business math and office machines. He found that he liked them. When he graduated, Peter applied for a job as a bank teller. Unfortunately, some applicants had more skills than he did.

"We do have a clerk position open," the manager said. "Then, if you can show us that you're organized and careful, we'll consider you for the next teller position."

Peter took the clerk job. He worked all day filing bank slips and checks. He didn't mind the routine nature of the work. However, he did wish that he could have more contact with customers. Peter did his work well. He also made sure the manager knew he still wanted to be a teller.

Finally a teller position opened up. Peter was hired. The bank put him through a training program. Peter really enjoyed his contact with the customers. More importantly, he continued to be careful with their money.

After several years, Peter took courses in how to prepare tax returns. He now plans to join a company that helps businesses prepare their tax returns. Peter's attention to detail and his good people skills will probably make him a success.

How to Learn More About Careers in the Office

By now, you know the first thing to do—research clerical jobs in the *Occupational Outlook Handbook.* Then talk with an office worker about his or her career. You can also do one or more of the following:

1. Volunteer to work in your school's office. Working even an hour a week will give you an idea of what office work can be like. You could also pick up some useful skills.

2. Work with a parent to help organize important papers at home. See how good you are at setting up a filing system. If doing this wouldn't be practical, set up a filing system for your own school work.

3. Go to an office supply store. Look at all the resources that businesses use to keep things organized. If they interest you, you might do well in an office career!

4. High schools sometimes offer courses in typing, word processing, business math, and bookkeeping. If you can, take at least one of these classes.

5. Look in the phone book under *Business Schools*. Find schools that specialize in training people to work in offices. Write to them for information about training in careers that interest you. You can also write to community colleges for information on business-related courses.

6. Write to one of the associations listed below for more information.

Office-Related Career Associations

Educational Institute of the American
  Hotel and Motel Association
1407 South Harrison Road
P.O. Box 1240
East Lansing, Michigan 48826

Communication Workers of America
1925 K Street, NW
Washington, DC 20006

Institute of Financial Education
111 East Wacker Drive
Chicago, IL 60601

Office and Professional Employees
  International Union
265 West 14th Street, Suite 610
New York, NY 10011

Professional Secretaries International
301 East Armour Boulevard
Kansas City, MO 64111

American Management Association
135 West 50th Street
New York, NY 10020

Chapter Review

Chapter Summary

- Office workers are also called *clerical workers*. They answer phones, greet customers, keep records, and handle shipments and deliveries of goods. They do almost anything that helps offices run smoothly.

- There are many types of office jobs. *Receptionists* greet and assist visitors and customers. *Record clerks* keep track of important paperwork, especially that which is related to money. *Shipping and receiving clerks* manage incoming and outgoing goods. *Secretaries* answer phones, type, and perform other office duties. *Word processors* enter documents into computers.

- The number of office jobs is expected to increase but at a slow rate. Technology will eliminate many jobs.

- Office workers should be careful and accurate and should like routine work. They must be willing to learn to operate office machines. People skills and math skills are helpful.

- Most office jobs provide routine lifestyles. Working hours are regular, usually from 8:00 A.M. to 5:00 P.M. Income depends on the type of work performed. The more skills an office worker has, the more he or she is likely to earn.

- To learn more about office jobs, volunteer in an office. Organize school and home projects. Learn about the equipment that is used in offices. Take a class in business math or office machines. Write to business schools and community colleges for information on classes and programs.

Chapter Quiz

Answer the following questions on a separate sheet of paper.

A. Thinking About Careers

1. What does a bookkeeper do?

2. What does a shipping and receiving clerk do?

3. What worker specializes in entering written information into a computer?

4. How might technology affect the need for word processors?

5. Who needs people skills more, a receptionist or a stock room clerk?

6. Who needs better math skills, a bookkeeper or a word processor?

7. If you like dressing up for work every day, should you apply for a job in an office or a warehouse?

8. What large machine might a stock clerk have to run?

9. Why do clerical supervisors usually earn more money than file clerks?

10. What is one project you could do to test your organizational skills?

B. Putting What You Learned to Work

Are your strengths and lifestyle choices suitable to an office career? Write a short explanation of why they are or are not. If you are interested in an office career, would you rather work in an office or in a warehouse? Why?

C. Work Out

Make a list of the strengths a bank teller should have. Rank them in order of importance. Discuss your answers with the class.

Chapter 10

Careers in the Trades

More women work in the trades today than have in the past.

Chapter Learning Objectives

- Identify two kinds of trade careers.
- Describe trends in trade careers.
- Match strengths and lifestyle choices to careers in the trades.
- List three ways to learn more about careers in the trades.

Words to Know

auto body worker a person who repairs car and truck bodies

auto mechanic a person who repairs the mechanical parts of cars and trucks

construction trades careers that involve the building of structures such as houses, highways, and bridges

contractor a person who manages building projects; the contractor usually hires workers as they are needed to complete the projects

craft guild an early organization of trade workers that was like a trade union

journeyman a skilled worker who has mastered a trade

machine trades careers that involve building, installing, running, and repairing machines

machinist a person who cuts, drills, and grinds metal into particular shapes and sizes

trade union an organized group of trade workers that attempts to get or maintain fair wages and working conditions for its members

It was Jenny's first day on the job. She was wearing blue jeans, a long-sleeved shirt, and a toolbelt. Her supervisor handed her a hardhat. "Put this on," he said. "I don't want a woman getting hurt on my work site." The supervisor turned away. Under his breath, Jenny heard him say, "Huh. A girl carpenter. She'll be more trouble than she's worth."

Jenny saw that she would have to prove her skills. All day long, she worked alongside the men to build the frame of a new house. She measured the wood carefully before cutting it. She nailed pieces together quickly. By the end of the day, she and her co-workers had almost finished the frame.

As Jenny packed up her tools, the supervisor spoke to her. "I've been watching you. You did a good job. Keep it up."

"Thanks," said Jenny. She began to walk away.

"By the way," said the supervisor, pointing. "I'll be getting rid of that sign."

Jenny looked. The sign read, "Men Working."

It had been a good day.

Careers in the Trades

Jenny is one of a growing number of women with careers in the trades. Trade workers are the builders of America. They build office buildings, bridges, tunnels, and machines. They lay water pipes. They wire buildings for electricity. They fix cars, mine coal, and drill for oil. Without such workers, the world would be a cold, dark place.

Many trade workers find careers in the **construction trades**. Construction workers make up the largest skilled work force in the United States. They build, repair, and remodel such structures as homes and highways.

Most workers in the construction trades do specialized jobs. Carpenters, for instance, might specialize in building homes, as Jenny did. They might also specialize in smaller items, such as cabinets or chairs. Bricklayers build walls, fireplaces, patios, and walkways with brick. Plumbers install pipes. Drywall workers put up walls made of sheetrock. Still other workers specialize in floor, roof, and tile work.

Skilled workers also find careers in the **machine trades**. This group includes people who build, install, maintain, and repair machines. Where would we be without the **auto mechanics** and **auto body workers** who fix our cars? **Machinists** spend their days cutting, drilling, and grinding metal into particular shapes and sizes. For example, some machinists shape large metal parts for airplanes. Others shape small pieces used in hand tools.

About one third of all construction workers are carpenters.

Job Trends in the Trades

Right now, about 4 million people in the United States work in the construction trade. That number is expected to grow to about 4.8 million by the year 2005. New jobs will be created by the need for new housing. Also, workers are always needed to maintain and repair aging highways, dams, bridges, and office buildings.

The outlook for many skilled workers in the machine trades is average to good. For example, good mechanics are always needed to repair cars and trucks. However, changes in the manufacturing industries could both hurt and help machine-trade workers. Foreign competition has caused some U.S. manufacturing plants to close. Some U.S. companies have moved their plants to countries where they can pay the workers less money. Each time a company leaves the United States, jobs here are lost. Some manufacturing plants are upgrading their machinery in order to produce more goods with fewer workers. These businesses will still need skilled workers to maintain the new machines.

Careers Practice

Answer these questions on a separate sheet of paper.

1. Name two occupations in the construction trade.

2. Name two occupations in the machine trade.

3. Are jobs in construction increasing greatly?

Are Your Strengths Right for a Career in the Trades?

When you see a sweaty worker hammering nails, you might not think of that worker as an artist. Many trade workers, however, do have artistic interests and skills. A woodworker, for example, might be called on to carve designs into wood. A stonemason might help create a beautiful garden walkway.

Trade workers should also have their share of mechanical skills. To do their jobs, they may need to operate both large and small tools. They may have to read blueprints and plans for buildings or machines.

As a rule, trade workers must be strong and healthy. People who work mainly with machines might not have as much heavy work to do as other trade workers. However, they may have to stand long hours on the job.

Workers in the trades like working with things. They like producing visible changes in the world. At the end of the day, they can point to a building or newly painted car and say, "Look what I've done!"

Careers in the Trades and Lifestyle Choices

Can you imagine crawling along a catwalk on the 35th floor of an unfinished building? Does the idea of working in rain, heat, or cold bother you? Would your family like you coming home each day with grease on your hands or sawdust in your hair?

You could have to experience these things if you had a career in the trades. Construction workers often work outside. Many machine-trade workers spend their days in noisy factories. It is more common to come home dirty than to come home clean. Workers in the trades dress for safety and comfort—not fashion.

What special problems do you think women face in the trades?

Historically, most trade jobs have been held by men. Things are changing, though. More and more women are now entering the trades. Many apprenticeship programs actively recruit women. On

Workers in the trades sometimes face dangerous conditions.

most job sites, however, the men still far outnumber the women.

Trade careers offer workers different employment options. Jenny the carpenter, for example, might own her own business. She might also get hired on an "as needed" basis by a **contractor** who manages projects. She could also be a full-time employee of a construction business.

Seasonal unemployment can be a problem for many construction workers. Most building is done in the dry months. In many parts of the country, few new buildings go up in the winter. Some workers continue earning money by working on indoor projects. Others have entirely different second careers during the winter months.

Beginning apprentices usually earn about half of what journeymen do.

There are a number of ways to learn a trade. Some businesses hire workers and then teach them a trade on the job. Many people seeking careers in the trades go through apprenticeship programs. Apprenticeship programs typically last from three to six years. During that time, the apprentice learns skills on the job. Classroom training is also provided. As skills are mastered, the apprentice works toward becoming a **journeyman**. Journeymen have mastered their trades. They get higher wages and better choices of jobs.

Many trade unions require workers to enter apprenticeship programs before they can become union members.

Skilled workers in the trades make good wages, especially if they are in **trade unions**. Trade unions are groups of skilled workers who organize for fair wages and working conditions. For certain jobs, large businesses often hire only union members. In 1990, the average pay for a machinist was around $27,000. Drywall workers earned between $19,950 and $49,900. A carpenter could earn as much as $35,000.

Apprenticeship programs are often run by unions.

Careers Practice

Answer these questions on a separate sheet of paper.

1. Should people with artistic interests consider working in a trade?

2. Who is more likely to work outside, a construction worker or a worker in the machine trades?

3. What do contractors do?

It's History: Unions

At the beginning of this century, a work day could last 14 hours. Factories hired young children to work for very low wages. Safety conditions were poor. Then workers banded together to form unions. Together, the union members worked for better wages and working conditions.

The great-grandparents of trade unions were called **craft guilds**. Craft guilds started in Europe in the 11th century. To fight competition, trade workers such as carpenters and goldsmiths joined together. They set standards for wages and work. The guilds lasted until about the 15th century. They then became outlawed in many countries.

The modern labor movement began in the United States in 1866 with the National Labor Union (NLU). That organization was formed to win an eight-hour work day for employees. The NLU was short-lived. Workers, however, would not give up. They created other unions and used strikes and other means to secure their rights. Today's workers owe much to the unions. This includes the eight-hour work day, the 40-hour work week, paid vacations, and sick leave.

How to Learn More About Careers in the Trades

Learning about careers in the trades isn't very difficult. Most of us have seen houses being built or know what a plumber does. As always, it is good to read about these careers. Apprenticeship programs,

Unions have used strikes to win better wages and working conditions.

community colleges, and vocational schools can also send you information. People who work in the trades are rather easy to find, too. Ask your family and friends for names of people to interview.

You can also use the following suggestions:

1. Take wood shop, machine shop, or auto shop if your school offers such classes. You'll learn to use tools for building and repair.

2. Read "how to" books on building. These books are usually written for homeowners, not carpenters or tile layers. However, they can give you a good idea of what skills are needed to do carpentry, drywall, tiling, and so on.

3. Use what you learn in school and the "how to" books to complete a home construction project. It

could be as small as fixing a leaky faucet. (You should be supervised by a parent or skilled worker.)

4. Get a part-time job in a hardware store. Hardware stores are great places to learn about "the tools of the trade." You will learn quickly about hammers, saws, nuts, bolts, paint, and more.

5. Get a summer job on a construction crew. See what it's like to work on a construction site. Days can be long and the work can be hard. You may like it! Your school counseling center or city employment office can help you apply.

6. Write to one of the associations listed below for more information.

In Chapter 3, you listed your accomplishments. Did any of them have to do with building something?

Trade Career Associations

Associated General Contractors of America
1957 E Street NW
Washington, DC 20006

International Union of Bricklayers and
Allied Craftsmen
815 15th Street, NW
Washington, DC 20005

American Council for Construction
Education
1015 15th Street, NW, Suite 700
Washington, DC 20005

United Brotherhood of Carpenters and
Joiners of America
101 Constitution Ave.
Washington, DC 20001

National Joint Painting, Decorating, and
Drywall Apprenticeship and Training
Committee
1750 New York Ave., NW, Lower Level
Washington, DC 20006

Technology Student Association
1914 Association Drive
Keston, VA 22091

Chapter Review

Chapter Summary

- Trade workers have built America's homes and businesses. Construction trade workers build houses, highways, bridges, and skyscrapers. Machine trade workers make, install, run, and repair machines. Workers in both groups tend to have specialized jobs.

- Jobs in the construction trades are expected to grow from about 4 million to 4.8 million by the year 2005. Machine trade jobs will be affected by trends in the manufacturing industry. Some jobs will be eliminated by the closing or moving of U.S. plants. Companies that upgrade their machines will still need skilled workers.

- Trade workers like working with their hands and with tools. They like to produce visible products.

- Trade workers may have to work in poor weather or in noisy factories. They dress for comfort and safety. Trade workers learn their crafts from other workers or through apprenticeship programs. Higher wages and better job choices often go to journeymen who are union members.

- To learn more about careers in the trades, take wood shop, machine shop, or auto shop classes. Read "how to" books on building. Do a home building project. Work at a hardware store or on a construction site.

Chapter Quiz

Answer the following questions on a separate sheet of paper.

A. Thinking About Careers

1. What small items could a carpenter specialize in making?

2. What does a drywall worker do?

3. What does a machinist do?

4. Are auto repairers in the machine trades or the construction trades?

5. When U.S. manufacturing plants close, how are workers in the machine trades affected?

6. Which person is more suited to the construction trade, someone with artistic interests or someone with scientific interests?

7. Joe loves to dress in the newest fashions. He hates to be seen with a single hair out of place. What would he not like about a career in the trades?

8. What is a journeyman?

9. What do trade unions try to obtain for their members?

10. What classes can a high school student take to learn more about the trades?

B. Putting What You Learned to Work

Are your strengths and lifestyle choices suitable to a career in the trades? Write a short explanation of why they are or are not.

C. Work Out

Imagine you are a construction worker. What kind of work do you do? What do you like most about your job? What do you like least?

Chapter 11

Careers in Sports and Entertainment

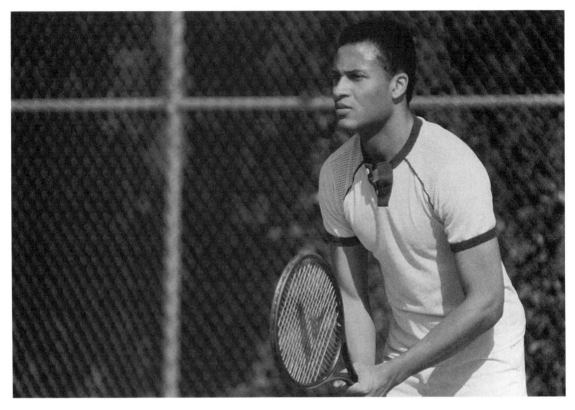

Careers in sports and entertainment require talent and discipline.

Chapter Learning Objectives

- Identify two kinds of sports and entertainment careers.
- Describe trends in sports and entertainment careers.
- Match strengths and lifestyle choices to sports and entertainment careers.
- List three ways to find out more about sports and entertainment careers.

Words to Know

comedian a person who tells jokes and funny stories in front of an audience

costume designer a worker who designs and sews clothing for performers in plays and movies

director a worker who coaches actors in a play or a movie

discipline training that develops character and self control

professional athlete a worker who is paid to perform sports in front of an audience

referee a worker who sees that rules are followed by the players during a sporting event such as a football or basketball game

scout a worker who looks for talented players and recommends that they be hired by another team

set designer a worker who designs and builds sets for movies and plays

umpire a worker who sees that the rules are followed by players during a baseball game

Jack and Leon played together on their high school tennis team. A big match was coming up on Friday.

"Come on, man," Jack said to Leon one afternoon. "Let's go practice. We'll never win if we don't."

"We can practice after school," Leon answered.

"We'll only have the court for an hour. If we skip last period, we'll have two whole hours of practice time."

"No way," said Leon, shaking his head.

Jack punched him in the arm. "I thought you wanted to be a professional. I thought you wanted to make millions of dollars. You'll never be a star at this rate. You don't have the drive to win."

Leon got angry. He grasped Jack's arm. "Look, Jack. If I don't graduate from high school, I'm going nowhere. My only chance to keep playing tennis is to go on to college. If my grades aren't high enough, I won't get in. Then all my dreams will go up in smoke."

Jack looked surprised. "Calm down, buddy. I'll meet you at the court after school. OK?"

Leon looked at his partner. "No harm done," he said. Inside, he wished Jack would think a little more about the future.

Careers in Sports and Entertainment

Leon is a practical young man. It's a good thing. He knows that anyone who wants to be a **professional athlete**—or entertainer—has a fight ahead of him or her. These fields are not impossible to have careers in. However, the odds of making it to the top are very slim.

How important is the role that professional referees and umpires play?

Fortunately, not everyone in sports has to be a professional athlete. Coaches, for example, help plan game strategy and improve players' skills. **Umpires** and **referees** watch games to see that the athletes play by the rules. Sports instructors coach people of all ages in how to play sports well.

The same goes for the entertainment field. Not everyone has to be a movie star, a top rock or rap musician, or a member of the New York City Ballet. **Costume designers** design and sew costumes for movies and plays. **Set designers** and carpenters build and paint sets. **Directors** plan productions and coach actors. Instructors help improve entertainers' skills. There are dozens of backstage careers that are exciting and creative.

Job Trends in Sports and Entertainment

Professional sports and entertainment are competitive job fields. Usually, there are many more applicants than positions.

Those who teach in these fields also face difficulties. Because of money problems, many schools are cutting back on sports, music, and drama programs.

The growing field of sports instruction does offer some hope for employment, though. More and more Americans are spending their leisure time learning and playing sports. Instructors are employed to teach private and group lessons. Health clubs, tennis clubs, golf courses, and community centers are all possible employers.

Careers Practice

Answer these questions on a separate sheet of paper.

1. Do costume designers work in sports or entertainment?

2. What do umpires and referees do?

3. As a rule, are the chances of becoming a top star in sports or entertainment good?

Are Your Strengths Right for a Career in Sports or Entertainment?

The odds for a top career in sports or entertainment aren't good. However, with the right strengths and good luck, people sometimes succeed.

It is very important that a person have raw talent. Most people know at an early age if they are athletic or not. Singers, actors, **comedians**, dancers, and other performing artists can judge their talent by comparing it to that of their peers. You need not be perfect. However, you must have at least an aptitude for what you want to do.

What special talent must a comedian have?

Desire and **discipline** are also important. A person must want the career badly enough to rehearse or work out over and over again. Olympic swimmers in training, for example, could spend up to eight hours a day doing nothing but swimming laps.

Maturity is also important. Athletes will sometimes lose important games. Entertainers will fail to find work. They must be able to learn from such unpleasant events.

People who want to coach or teach must be patient. Their task will not always be to win, but to help others.

Careers and Lifestyle Choices

To win the rewards of a career in sports or entertainment, a person must spend hours in practice or rehearsal. Travel is often part of the job. Days and months could be spent on the road or away from home.

Athletes and dancers are always at risk of injury. Knee surgery is common among workers in both these careers. Some athletes become disabled in their later years from the many hits they took when younger.

Athletes and dancers are at risk of injury.

To get good training and to be "seen," athletes usually must attend college after high school. College coaches take a young person's abilities and develop them further. **Scouts** watch college games regularly and recommend players to professional teams. It is possible for very talented high school athletes to go straight into professional sports. However, it is very unlikely. Going to college has another benefit. Most athletes have brief careers. College allows them to prepare for careers after sports.

Workers in the performing arts can also get training at colleges and specialized schools. Some would-be entertainers choose to take private lessons. Still others work part-time at paying jobs and entertain part-time at non-paying jobs.

The payoffs for workers in sports and entertainment could be great or small. For example, players in the National Football League earned an average of $175,000 per year in 1990. Major-league baseball players earned an average of $300,000 per year. A few top tennis players earn in the millions.

As you may have guessed, high school coaches are not *quite* as well paid. They typically earn between $20,000 and $30,000 per year. Sports instructors could earn between $6 and $75 per hour. The rate depends on how skilled they are, the sport they teach, and where they work.

Workers in the entertainment world are in a similar position. Top stars earn millions. However, there are few top stars. Wage standards for entertainers are usually set by unions. One survey reports that 80 percent of the actors registered in unions do not make enough money to live on. At least 30 percent make no money at all in an entire year! Even those who do get work do not earn a great deal. The average salary for screen actors in the early 1990s was $10,400 per year.

To be accepted by the Professional Golfers Association, you must pass both a written and an oral test. Of course, you must also be a skilled golfer!

In the early 1990s, ballet dancers made about $220 per performance.

In 1990, over 80 percent of the members of the Actors' Equity Association and the Screen Actors Guild earned $5,000 or less.

Careers Practice

Answer these questions on a separate sheet of paper.

1. What strength is most needed by someone who wants a career in sports or entertainment?

2. Where do athletes usually go for training after high school?

3. How much do high school coaches typically earn?

A choir is one place to get musical training.

Close Up: Making It In Music

Ever since Lila was a child, she had wanted to sing. When she was ten, she joined her church choir. Soon she was singing solos and being praised by church members for her voice.

Throughout junior high and high school, Lila continued to sing. She sang in school musicals. She performed at friends' parties. She and two other students formed a pop singing group.

When she finished high school, Lila didn't have enough money to go to college right away. However, she was determined to have a career in music. She now works during the week selling instruments in a music store. On weekends, she performs at local clubs or at weddings. On Sundays she leads the church choir. She hopes to save enough to get a degree in music or at least to take private lessons.

Is she tired?

"Not really," says Lila. "I get energy from performing. It's not even that important that I become a star. I'm doing what I love. That's what keeps me going."

How to Learn More About Careers in Sports and Entertainment

As you do your research, keep an open mind. People who work backstage and on the sidelines also have exciting careers. Do these activities as part of your research.

1. If you feel you have some talent, then practice, practice, practice. Set routines and stick with them.

Find out if you have the discipline to pursue a career in sports or entertainment.

2. Go to the theater. Try out for school plays. Take classes in the performing arts. Or become involved in sports. Cross-training in different sports is often advised by sports trainers. If you are a football player, think about taking ballet as well!

3. Here's a tough one: watch TV. Tune in to whatever interests you: sports, dance, acting, or music. Don't just watch. Study what the performers or athletes are doing. Try to apply the techniques that you see.

4. Volunteer to coach others at a church, community recreation center, or senior center. You will discover if you have the patience and desire to teach or coach others.

5. Read biographies (life stories) of famous people in the field you are exploring. Learn what it took for them to succeed.

6. Write to one of the associations listed below for more information.

Sports and Entertainment Associations

American Alliance for Health,
   Physical Education, Recreation, and Dance
1900 Association Drive
Reston, VA 22091

The Athletic Institute
200 Castlewood Drive
North Palm Beach, FL 33408

Screen Actors Guild
7065 Hollywood Blvd.
Hollywood, CA 90028

American Dance Guild
31 West 21st Street, 3rd Floor
New York, NY 10010

National Endowment for the Arts
1100 Pennsylvania Ave., NW
Washington, DC 29506

American Guild of Musical Artists
1727 Broadway, Suite 1269
New York, NY 10105

Chapter Review

Chapter Summary

- There are many different careers in sports and entertainment. Professional athletes need coaches, trainers, umpires, and referees. Dancers, musicians, and actors work with directors, coaches, costume designers, and set designers. Careers backstage and on the sidelines can be exciting and rewarding.

- In these fields, there will probably always be more applicants than there are jobs. Public school coaching jobs have been harder to find due to budget cuts. Those interested in teaching sports may find job opportunities in health clubs.

- People who want careers in sports or entertainment must have talent. Discipline and the ability to bounce back from disappointment are also important strengths.

- People who make it big in entertainment and sports are rewarded with fame and high incomes. But they spend many hours practicing and traveling. Most people in these fields earn low to average incomes.

- To learn about these careers, keep practicing. Take classes. Study related events on TV. Volunteer to teach others. Read biographies of successful sports and entertainment figures.

Chapter Quiz

Answer these questions on a separate sheet of paper.

A. Thinking About Careers

1. What are professional athletes paid to do?

2. What do costume designers do?

3. What do directors do?

4. As a rule, what are a person's chances of becoming a star?

5. Why must athletes and entertainers have discipline?

6. As a rule, are careers in sports and entertainment suitable for people who hate to travel?

7. What do athletes and dancers always risk?

8. Who makes a higher average salary, professional football players or baseball players?

9. Do most actors make good incomes?

10. How can watching TV help you learn more about careers in sports and entertainment?

B. Putting What You Learned to Work

Are your strengths and lifestyle choices suitable to a career in sports or entertainment? Write a short explanation of why they are or are not.

C. Work Out

Well-known athletes and entertainers often complain that they have no privacy. If you were famous, how would want to be treated by fans and the press? Write a short explanation.

Unit Three Review

Answer these questions on a separate sheet of paper.

1. What will you find in the *Occupational Outlook Handbook*?

2. What can you learn by doing an informational interview?

3. Are jobs in health care increasing or decreasing?

4. Why do sales workers need strong persuasive skills?

5. What does a receptionist do?

6. What is the outlook for robotics technicians?

7. Why will there always be a need for workers in the construction trades?

8. What is a journeyman?

9. What strengths do workers in sports and entertainment need?

10. Of all the careers you read about in Unit Three, which interests you the most? Why?

Unit Four

More Careers to Consider

Chapter 12

A Career as an Entrepreneur

Entrepreneurs organize and run their own businesses.

Chapter Learning Objectives

- List three ways to become an entrepreneur.
- Describe trends in entrepreneurship.
- Match strengths and lifestyle choices to a career as an entrepreneur.
- List three ways to find out more about becoming an entrepreneur.

Words to Know

capital any money or equipment invested in running a business

entrepreneur a person who organizes and runs a business

facsimile machine a machine that sends written documents over the phone lines; also called a *fax machine*

franchise an arrangement between an entrepreneur and a business chain. The entrepreneur pays to use the chain's name and to sell its products or services.

independent not influenced or controlled by others

investor a person who loans money to a business with the hope of making a profit

profit the money made by a business after all its costs have been paid

---

Paul walked into the house after school. The smell of cookies filled the air. "Julie must be baking," he thought. He rushed to the kitchen.

"Hey, Sis," Paul said to Julie as he put his arm around her. "How about a cookie?"

Paul looked down at the plate on the counter. It was filled with strangely shaped cookies of all colors. Not one was like another.

"What kind of cookies are these?" Paul asked, picking one up with care. "It looks like something from outer space."

Julie laughed. "I call them 'Kookies.' They're my latest invention. I'm going to sell them at the school fair. I'm betting that people will buy them because they look weird. If I'm right, I just might become the next Famous Amos. He's made millions with his chocolate-chip cookie recipe."

Paul took a bite of the cookie. It tasted pretty good. "Kooky Cookies. Not a bad idea, Sis. Let me know if I can help."

Julie slapped her brother's hand as he reached for another. "You can help by not eating the profits!"

Career Options for Entrepreneurs

Julie is taking her first steps toward becoming an entrepreneur. An **entrepreneur** is a person who organizes and runs a business. Entrepreneurs try to make profits with their businesses. **Profit** is the money left over after all the costs of doing business have been paid.

America's economy was built on the ideas and hard work of its entrepreneurs. Some of America's first entrepreneurs were fur trappers. They made money by selling wild animal furs. Henry Ford was a famous American entrepreneur. He was the first person to use an assembly line to manufacture cars. An entrepreneur probably owns your neighborhood grocery store or the hot dog cart on the corner.

People who want careers as entrepreneurs have several options. Many entrepreneurs start businesses from scratch. They develop an idea or find a need and then turn it into a product or service. Julie was doing this with her "Kookies." She thought more people would buy her cookies if she made them unusual.

Entrepreneurs also have the option of buying businesses that are already in place. For example, Ms. Falachi, the owner of a neighborhood pizza shop, decides to retire. She puts up her business for sale. Mr. Sherman, an entrepreneur, buys the restaurant and all its equipment. Then Mr. Sherman might try to improve the business. He might change the name, install a large-screen TV, or add more cheese to the pizza.

Other entrepreneurs choose to buy franchises. A **franchise** is a business arrangement between an entrepreneur and a large business chain. The

Ninety percent of American businesses are considered "small businesses."

Businesses started "from scratch" are sometimes called *start-up companies*.

business chain allows the entrepreneur to use its name and to sell its products or services. In exchange, the entrepreneur pays the chain a fee. Entrepreneurs usually risk less when buying a franchise than when starting an entirely new business. The larger company usually provides training and helps the new owner in other ways. In addition, buyers are probably already familiar with the franchise's product. McDonald's is one of the most famous American franchises.

Career Trends for Entrepreneurs

In 1991, almost nine million workers in the United States were their own bosses. Entrepreneurs make up at least 7.7 percent of the total work force. That number has been growing since the 1970s. Why?

The increase is partly due to recessions. Remember that during a recession, businesses produce fewer goods and services. As a result, fewer workers are needed and more people lose their jobs. During the late 1980s and early 1990s, the United States was in a long recession. To survive, many companies became smaller.

Some of the workers who lost their jobs during the recession decided to try new careers. They became entrepreneurs. Many of them sold their services back to the companies that had fired them. For example, John, a computer programmer, was fired from a large firm. He started his own business in computer repair. Among his clients is the company he once worked for full-time.

Technology is another reason why the number of entrepreneurs is growing. Computers and **facsimile (fax) machines** make it less expensive to set up home offices. John, the programmer, does all his own bookkeeping on his computer. He sends out bills by fax. He even orders computer parts for his business

What other kinds of businesses could be run from a home?

with his computer. The new technology allows him to be better organized and to do more work. This is very important for small businesses.

Careers Practice

Answer these questions on a separate sheet of paper.

1. What is an entrepreneur?

2. Name one example of a franchise.

3. Is the number of entrepreneurs increasing?

Are Your Strengths Right for a Career as an Entrepreneur?

Sharon is a good example of an entrepreneur. She noticed that many people in her neighborhood rented home videos on the weekends. She also noticed that many of them forgot to return the movies to the video store on time. As a result, the renters had to pay late fees.

Sharon got an idea. She would start a home video delivery service. For one dollar plus the rental fee, Sharon would pick up and deliver the video of a customer's choice. The next day she would return the video to the store. The dollar she charged her customers would be less than any late fees they might otherwise have to pay. If Sharon could get ten customers every Friday and Saturday, she'd have a nice weekend job.

At first, the idea sounded good. Then Sharon realized that all the videos would be rented in her name. If for some reason a video was not returned on time, *she* would pay the late fee. If the video was damaged or lost, *she* would have to pay for it. Going

If you were Sharon, would you go ahead with the plan? Why or why not?

into business meant that Sharon would be risking her savings. Yet, after much thought, she decided to go ahead with her plan.

Sharon has the strengths of an entrepreneur. Entrepreneurs watch the world and the people around them. They devise ideas for new or improved goods and services. Entrepreneurs are also risk-takers. They are willing to risk their own money or the money of **investors** to make a business succeed.

Entrepreneurs are usually **independent** people with lots of confidence. They are not afraid to make decisions on their own. They are also willing and able to learn many new things. As her business's only employee, Sharon will have to be owner, salesperson, office manager, and delivery person. She will have to learn about business licenses, taxes, and insurance. Very importantly, she will have to find out how to promote her business. She will need to make people aware of her business. She'll need to make them want to use her service. If the business grows, Sharon will have to learn how to train and manage others.

Entrepreneurs like challenges.

Lifestyle Choices for Entrepreneurs

An entrepreneur can start a business just about anywhere. Many have businesses in their homes. Others rent or buy property where they can set up factories or sale rooms. Some entrepreneurs travel frequently. Others work entirely from their offices.

Can an entrepreneur work outside? Of course! Gardeners who own their own businesses are entrepreneurs. Some entrepreneurs drive trucks or build houses. The nature of their businesses determines where they spend their time.

It is not unusual for an entrepreneur to work 12-hour days. To save money, the owner of a new business may do the work of many people. Even after a business grows, an entrepreneur may spend long days making sure it runs smoothly.

Entrepreneurs do not necessarily need special education or training. However, an entrepreneur must have good ideas and be a good planner. Business courses can help any entrepreneur be better prepared. Entrepreneurs can also learn about running successful businesses from other business owners.

Many entrepreneurs start businesses believing they'll become fantastically rich. This doesn't happen often. About one fourth of all new businesses fail within three years. One reason for this is that many businesses start without enough capital. **Capital** is the money and equipment that is invested in running a business. Julie, for example, needs money to buy cookie ingredients. She also needs a stove to bake the cookies.

Capital could come from an entrepreneur's savings. The entrepreneur could also borrow money from banks or investors. It may take many years to pay the money back. Experts say that it takes up to five years for most businesses to make a profit.

No entrepreneur is guaranteed a high income. In 1988, the average income of a business owned by one person was $13,871 per year. Still, with all its hardships, many people find that being an entrepreneur is quite rewarding. Entrepreneurs often value their independence more than they value high incomes. It is a career choice that must be made carefully.

Capital is any money or equipment used to run a business.

Careers Practice

Answer these questions on a separate sheet of paper.

1. Why should entrepreneurs be confident?

2. How many new businesses fail?

3. Do all entrepreneurs become rich?

One resource for entrepreneurs is the Small
Business Administration (SBA). The SBA is an
independent agency of the federal government.
It loans money to small businesses. It assists
businesses in getting government contracts. It
provides information on how to run a business
successfully.

Are you interested in starting a business? Go
to your library and take a look at the two-
volume *Small Business Handbook*. Let's say you
wanted to start a bakery business. Under
Bakery/Donut Shop, you would find dozens of
resources helpful to someone who wanted to
start, buy, or run such a business. Volume Two
of the handbook lists important small business
resources by state.

How to Learn More About Becoming an Entrepreneur

There is no listing in the *Occupational Outlook
Handbook* for "entrepreneur." However, there are
hundreds of books, articles, and even videos on
starting and running your own business. Use these
tools to learn as much as you can. Then find someone
who owns a business. Many people in the trades are
self-employed. You might also try small businesses in
your neighborhood. Interview the person. Learn if you
have the strengths and desire it takes to become an
entrepreneur.

Here are some other activities that may help you:

1. On your own or with a group of friends, brainstorm
   ideas for new or improved products and services.

Try thinking about a product you like. Could it be made even better? Then think about a product you don't like. Could you improve it? Such exercises will get you thinking like an entrepreneur.

2. Join an entrepreneurs' training program for people in your age group. (Junior Achievement is one of the best-known.) Students in these groups start and run their own businesses. Your school counselor or community librarian can help you find one.

3. Take an economics class if your school offers one. Many economics classes include important lessons on business ownership, budgeting, and other important skills.

4. Call or write your local chamber of commerce. Ask for a list of small independent businesses in your area. You will get some idea of the many types of businesses run by entrepreneurs.

5. Come up with an idea for a business. If it really excites you, plan how to make it a reality. Talk over your plans with a parent, teacher, or other adult. If the idea still seems good, go for it! Work hard to be a success.

6. Write to one of the associations listed below for more information:

Associations for Entrepreneurs

The Small Business Administration
409 Third Street, NW
Washington, DC 20416

American Entrepreneurs Association
2392 Morse Avenue
Irvine, CA 92714

Association of Collegiate Entrepreneurship
Box 147
Wichita State University
Wichita, KS 67208

Minority Business Development Agency
Herbert Clark Hoover Building, Room 6707
14th Street and Constitution Ave, NW
Washington, DC 20230

Business Assistance Service
Office of Business Liaison
U.S. Department of Commerce, Room 5898-C
Washington, DC 20203

Chapter Summary

- *Entrepreneurs* are people who organize and run their own businesses. Entrepreneurs sometimes start their own businesses from the ground up. Sometimes they buy businesses or franchises.

- The number of entrepreneurs in the United States is growing. Many of the newest entrepreneurs are workers who lost their jobs.

- New tools such as home computers and facsimile machines allow entrepreneurs to run their businesses more easily.

- Entrepreneurs are risk-takers. They are confident and independent, and they like challenges.

- Entrepreneurs must be willing and able to learn many different tasks.

- Where an entrepreneur works depends on the nature of his or her business. As a rule, entrepreneurs work long hours. Usually they do not make large incomes.

- To learn about being an entrepreneur, try thinking like one. Come up with ideas for new or improved products and services. Take economics classes. Join entrepreneur training organizations. Learn about businesses in your community. Plan your own business!

Chapter Quiz

Answer these questions on a separate sheet of paper.

A. Thinking About Careers

1. What is a person who organizes and runs a business called?

2. What are three ways for an entrepreneur to get started in business?

3. Explain how a recession can affect the number of entrepreneurs.

4. What two pieces of equipment have helped many entrepreneurs start home offices?

5. What do entrepreneurs risk when starting businesses?

6. Do entrepreneurs have to be good decision-makers?

7. Where do entrepreneurs usually work?

8. After three years, what happens to 25 percent of new small businesses?

9. What was the average 1988 income of businesses owned by one person?

10. What subjects might a person would-be entrepreneur study?

B. Putting What You Learned to Work

Are your strengths and lifestyle choices suitable to a career as an entrepreneur? Write a short explanation of why they are or are not.

C. Work Out

John often goes to baseball games in the summer. He sits in the bleachers, where the seats are cheaper. One thing John hates about going to these games is how hot it gets. Wearing a hat just makes him sweat more. Can you think of any product or service to offer people with this problem? How would you sell it?

Chapter 13

A Career as a Homemaker and Parent

Babysitting is one way to learn the skills needed for parenting.

Chapter Learning Objectives

- Explain how homemaking and parenting are careers.
- Describe important family trends.
- Match strengths and lifestyle choices to becoming a homemaker and parent.
- List three ways to learn more about homemaking and parenting.

Words to Know

budget   a plan of how to balance income and spending

homemaker   a person who manages a household

parent   a person who has the long-term responsibility of raising a child

poverty line   the minimum yearly income that a family must have in order to meet its basic needs

Nancy had found a summer job babysitting twin eight-year-old boys. At noon each day, she would walk them home from summer camp. In the afternoon, she'd keep the boys busy, clean the house, and start supper. Her employer, Rita Palmer, was a single parent who worked outside the home.

At first, Nancy liked her new job. She felt grown-up. Then she found out how much energy it takes to run a house and care for a family. The boys, who had enjoyed her company, also changed. They began to test her.

"You're not our mother. You can't tell us what to do," they would say. One day, Nancy lost her temper. She yelled at the boys and then began to cry. That evening, she sat down with Rita.

"I'm not sure I can do this job," Nancy confessed. "I'm spending too much time just getting the boys to listen to me. I can't seem to keep the house neat and keep them busy, too."

Rita patted Nancy's hand. "There's an old saying— 'Kids don't come with instructions.' The boys are a challenge, I know that. Let me explain what I do to get them to mind me. I should have given you some pointers before you started the job."

Nancy used the tips that Rita Palmer gave her. Usually they worked.

"I never thought about it before," Nancy told her father. "I guess it takes time to learn how to take care of children."

Who Are the Homemakers and Parents?

Nancy is getting an idea of what it's like to be a homemaker and parent. A **homemaker** is a person who manages a household. A homemaker may or may not also be a parent. A **parent** is a person who has the long-term responsibility of raising a child. Most people become parents by naturally producing a child. Other parents adopt their children. While it takes two parents to produce a child, two people do not always raise it. Sometimes, one parent dies or leaves the family.

For a long time, people didn't think being a homemaker or parent was really a "career." Someone had to take care of the household. Someone had to care for the children. In most cases, it was the role of the wife in the family.

Times have changed. Family planning now allows men and women to choose when they will have children. Fathers are taking a more active role in raising their children. Women have more opportunities to work outside the home. People now see that being a homemaker and a parent are jobs that require certain strengths that not everyone has or wishes to develop. In this sense, being a homemaker and parent is a career.

Older dictionaries give this definition for *homemaker*: "A woman who manages a home. Housewife."

Family Trends

At one time, the words "American family" brought to mind the picture of a husband, a wife, and two or three children. The husband had a career outside the home. The wife stayed home to cook, clean, and raise the children.

Many families of the 1990s do not match this picture. In 58 percent of the families with children under 18, both the mother and the father work outside the home. Many parents have two careers—one outside the home and one as a parent.

One reason why more mothers are working is that women have more opportunities than they once did. Different career fields are now more open to women. However, the state of today's economy also causes many mothers to work outside the home. Housing and health care are expensive. Raising a family on one income is difficult. Working mothers provide important second incomes.

Raising a family is even harder for single mothers. In the United States, 43 percent of single-parent families are headed by women who fall below the **poverty line**. They earn less than the minimum yearly income that a family must have to meet its basic needs. Yet the number of women who become single mothers is increasing. In 1950, four percent of all children were born to unmarried mothers. In 1990, the figure was close to 26 percent.

It is predicted that by 1995, two thirds of children under six will have mothers who are employed.

On average, women earn 72 cents to every dollar earned by men.

Careers Practice

Answer these questions on a separate sheet of paper.

1. What does a homemaker do?

2. Is the number of mothers with children in the work force increasing or decreasing?

3. What is the poverty line?

Parenting classes teach basic care skills. They also teach parents how to cope with stress in a healthy way.

Are Your Strengths Right for a Career as a Homemaker and Parent?

What does it take to be a good parent?

There is no easy answer to this question. There are many different styles of parenting. Some parents are strict. Others are easy with their children. A parent may raise two children in just the same way and see them turn out very differently.

There are, however, some basic strengths that can help any parent. First of all, a person should have a liking for infants and small children. Spending time with a baby is very different from being with teenagers or adults. A six-month-old cannot discuss sports or the latest fashions. A two-year-old will be more interested in playing with blocks than watching MTV. In many ways, parents are a child's first teachers. They must put aside their interests to help the child learn. Being patient, persuasive, and creative helps with this task.

Knowing how to handle stress is also a key skill for parents. Many parents will tell you that having children is a wonderful experience. Most will also tell you how demanding children can be. Newborn babies may wake up every two hours to be fed. A sick child could cry for hours at a time. A normal two-year-old will throw temper tantrums, hit, kick, and scream for what seems like no reason at all. (And you know how much trouble teenagers can be!) All this may be in addition to the normal problems and pressures of everyday life. Parents should know how to cope with the stress, anger, and other natural feelings that this type of behavior can cause. If they can't cope, they're at risk of hurting themselves or their children.

Parents must also be good planners. They must be able to budget money. A **budget** is a plan of how to balance income and spending. A parent must be able to provide food, clothing, shelter, and health care to his or her family. It can be difficult.

Lifestyle Choices for Homemakers and Parents

A full-time homemaker and parent will spend most of his or her time in the family house or apartment. Working parents will also spend most of their free time at home. Regular housekeeping tasks include cooking, cleaning, and paying bills. Parents will also have to change diapers, give baths, and read stories to their young children. Many of these tasks are routine.

Parenting is a full-time job with plenty of overtime. It doesn't really include "days off." Even when they're by themselves and away from home, parents may worry about their children.

One of the most important choices working parents will have to make has to do with child care. Children may be left with relatives, or babysitters may come to the home. Some parents leave their children in day-care centers. When making these choices, parents must consider location, cost, and the care their children will receive.

Becoming a parent does not require any special education or training. However, as Nancy learned at the beginning of this chapter, children don't come with instructions. Now parents can get help. Many hospitals, schools, and community agencies offer parenting classes. Classes for new parents usually focus on the basic skills of feeding, clothing, and caring for a newborn. Other parenting classes teach how to discipline children. Still others teach how to choose child care or handle the stresses of being a parent. These classes can be helpful to parents of any age.

People considering a career as parents should also think about income. Raising children can be costly. Experts say it costs roughly $100,000 to raise a child from birth to the age of 18!

Watching a child learn and grow can be a wonderful and challenging experience. It is also a big responsibility and one that should be chosen with care.

Careers Practice

Answer these questions on a separate sheet of paper.

1. List three things that can cause a parent stress.

2. Name one place that could offer parenting classes.

3. What is the average cost of raising a child?

Learn More About It: Stopping Child Abuse

Here are the sad facts:

- Over one million children are severely abused each year. Over one thousand of these will die. Quite often, the children are abused by their own parents.
- Children who survive abuse may face tough problems as they grow older. A recent study found that 68 percent of the juvenile lawbreakers in Oregon came from violent homes.
- At least 30 percent of the children who come from violent homes will grow up to become abusers. They will repeat the behavior they learned as children.

How do we break the cycle? In many cases, parenting classes can help. After all, abusers learned how to be violent. They can also *unlearn* it. We can find out how to handle stress and anger without drugs, alcohol, or violence.

If you're interested in finding parenting classes, you can call your county social services department. The local YMCA and your nearby library can usually provide referrals, too.

How to Learn More About Being a Homemaker and Parent

Will you find a listing for "parent" in the *Dictionary of Occupational Titles*? No, but don't let that stop you from doing your research. You probably know dozens of parents to interview. Ask about the challenges and rewards of parenting. Find out what skills are needed to manage a household.

No one becomes a parent knowing how to do it. However, the following can help you learn something about the subject:

1. Find a part-time job as a babysitter or child care worker. Try different age groups. Test your patience and creativity in these jobs.

2. If you can't find a paying job, try volunteering in a preschool or kindergarten. Talk to the teacher about what kinds of things children need to learn and grow.

3. Take home economics or consumer economics classes in school. These classes will help you learn how to budget, shop wisely, and do other household tasks.

4. Ask a parent to explain your family's budget. Find out how much it costs to raise a child and run a household. Consider rent, clothing, food, phone, and other expenses.

5. Research the parenting classes in your community. Hospitals, YMCAs, and libraries are good places to start. Call the instructor and ask if you can attend a class. Share what you learn with your friends and family.

6. Look up the topics "parenting," "parent education," and "child care" in your library catalog. Find books and articles on a subject that interests you and read them. Use what you learn to help you now or in the future.

7. Write or call the following organizations for more information.

Parent Education Resources

Family Resources Coalition
200 South Michigan Avenue, Suite 1520
Chicago, IL 60604

Planned Parenthood Federation of America
810 7th Avenue
New York, NY 10019

Parent Effectiveness Training (PET)
1-800-628-1197

Systematic Training for Effective Parenting*
(STEP)

Active Parenting*

*Look in your phone book for addresses and phone numbers of local chapters of these organizations.

Chapter Review

Chapter Summary

- At one time, being a homemaker and raising children was seen as the responsibility of the wife in a family. Now fathers are more active in raising children. Also, women have more opportunities to work outside the home.

- Family planning allows people to choose when they will have children. With this choice comes a life-long responsibility. In this way being a homemaker and a parent is a career choice.

- In more than half of the American families with children, both the mother and the father work outside the home. The number of single-parent families is growing in this country as well. Some 43 percent of the single-parent families headed by women live below the poverty line.

- People considering careers as parents should like being with and teaching children. They must know how to handle stress. It also helps if they are good planners. Homemakers must budget, plan meals, and take care of many family needs.

- Parenting takes a *lot* of time. It also takes a lot of money. It costs about $100,000 to raise a child from birth to the age of 18. There are no education requirements for being a parent. However, many parenting classes are now teaching basic skills.

- To learn more about being a homemaker and parent, a person could work or volunteer with children. Home economics, consumer economics, and parenting classes may be helpful. There are also many books and articles written for parents.

Chapter Quiz

Answer the following questions on a separate sheet of paper.

A. Thinking About Careers

1. Do people now have a choice about whether or not to become parents?

2. In most American families, is there one parent at home all the time taking care of children?

3. What are two reasons why more and more mothers work outside the home?

4. About what percentage of families headed by single women fall below the poverty line?

5. Why is it important for parents to know how to handle stress and anger?

6. Why should parents be good planners?

7. What are some of the things parents must provide for their children?

8. Where do parents spend most of their "free" time?

9. How can parenting classes help abusive parents?

10. Where can a person work or volunteer to learn more about what it takes to be a parent?

B. Putting What You Learned to Work

At this time in your life, do you think you have the strengths it takes to be a parent? Does the lifestyle of a parent suit you? How might that change as you get older? Explain.

C. Work Out

Write a list of reasons to become a parent. Then write a list of reasons not to become a parent. Compare your lists with those of a classmate.

Chapter 14

Working for the Government

These people are employed by the government. They are paid with tax dollars.

Chapter Learning Objectives

- Describe the kinds of jobs to be found in government service.
- Describe trends in government employment.
- Match your strengths and lifestyle choices to government work.
- List three ways to find out more about government work.

Words to Know

appoint   to choose a person for a particular job or task

bureaucracy   an organization that has many levels and that has strict ways of doing things

civil service   the system that hires workers for government jobs

disability   the condition of not being able to do something

elect   to choose by voting

electrician   a person who sets up or fixes electrical equipment

local government   the level of government that manages counties, cities, and towns

mechanic   a person who makes, repairs, or uses machines

military personnel   the people who serve in a country's armed forces

recruiter   a person who gets others to join an organization such as a branch of the armed forces

retire   to leave a job or career, usually because of age

Every Friday in Mr. Larson's career education class, a guest speaker would talk about his or her career. One Friday, three speakers stood before the class. Mr. Larson introduced them. The first speaker was a police dispatcher. He informed police officers over the radio about crimes, accidents, and other emergencies. The second speaker taught kindergarten classes. The third speaker was in the army. She worked as a **mechanic**.

"Well, class," said Mr. Larson. "Before we go any further, I want you to tell me what these jobs have in common."

The class was quiet. "Uh, they get paid?" one of the students finally said.

Mr. Larson and the speakers laughed. "Well, that's true. But what they really have in common is *who* pays them. All three of these people work for the government. Your tax dollars pay their salaries. They work for *you*!"

Who Works for the Government?

Tax dollars pay the salaries of over 21 million government workers. In fact, the government is the largest employer in the United States.

When we say "the government," what do we mean? Workers are employed by three levels of government. The federal government, centered in Washington, D.C., employs people in 110 agencies around the world. For example, people who work for the U.S. Postal Service are federal employees. The 50 state governments employ over four million workers. The rangers in your state parks are state employees. The more than 83,000 **local governments** include cities, counties, townships, and other special districts. Police officers, fire fighters, street cleaners, and teachers are all employed by local governments.

Government workers fall into three basic groups. **Civil service** employees are hired by particular departments or agencies. Some of these jobs are quite specialized and are found only in the government. For example, fire fighters provide a service that is not offered by private businesses. However, thousands of civil service jobs are identical to jobs found in private businesses. The government employs office workers, trade workers, health workers, and more.

Military personnel work for the armed forces. Instead of being hired, they enlist in, or join, the army, navy, air force, marines, and coast guard. People in the armed forces strive to protect and defend the country. To do this, they train in many different careers. Radio operator, computer technician, **electrician**, and dental assistant are some of the jobs found in the armed forces.

Elected and appointed officials are the third group of government employees. This group is fairly small. It includes about half a million paid workers. Mayors, governors, and the president of the United States are

About one in four workers in the armed forces holds a technical job that involves machines or electronic equipment.

About 52 percent of workers at the state and local levels work in education.

in this category. Citizens vote or **elect** them into office. These elected officials can then choose or **appoint** people to certain jobs. For example, a city's mayor appoints its police chief. Unlike civil service employees, appointed officials do not have to take tests for their jobs.

Trends in Government Employment

From 1950 to 1980, the number of government jobs greatly increased. The baby boom, which began after World War II, was partly responsible for this. As the

In the 1980s and early 1990s, many education budgets were cut.

population grew, more government services were needed. Schools were built and roads were paved. Teachers and construction crews were hired.

Beginning in 1980, however, things began to change. Recessions and lower taxes meant that governments took in less money. To meet their budgets, some agencies had to cut employees and services. At the state and local levels, the worst cuts were seen in education.

The breaking up of the Soviet Union has also affected federal employment. After World War II, the Soviet Union was seen as a threat to the United States. Military spending was increased, even during the 1980s, when other agencies' budgets were cut. From 1980 to 1989, employment in the Department of Defense went up 11 percent.

With the end of the Soviet Union in 1991, U.S. government leaders saw the opportunity to cut defense spending. By the late 1990s, all branches of the military except the coast guard plan to have cut back their personnel by about 25 percent. Nearly 70 military bases are scheduled to close.

Still, career experts say that the outlook for civil service jobs and military positions is good. Every year, thousands of people **retire**, get fired, or leave government jobs. Some of these jobs will be cut, but many will still need to be filled. Public schools, police departments, and the armed forces will not disappear. It is likely that the government will continue to be the country's largest employer for many years to come.

Careers Practice

Answer these questions on a separate sheet of paper.

1. What are the three levels of government?

2. What level of government employs police officers?

3. How has the breakup of the Soviet Union affected military employment?

Are Your Strengths Right for a Career in the Government?

Most government jobs have counterparts in private business. A secretary working at City Hall needs the same skills as a secretary working for a private company. However, there are some important differences between government agencies and private businesses. Businesses exist to make profits. Government agencies are not for profit. They exist to provide services. Social services agencies help people get food and shelter. Police departments fight crime. Public works departments build and maintain roads. The Department of Education tries to educate students. The interests, skills, and knowledge needed to be hired by these agencies vary greatly. However, the happiest workers in these agencies share one important strength. They value the missions of the departments they work for.

Another strength that most government workers share is patience. Getting a civil service job can be a long process. To get a civil service job, you must first fill out an application. Qualified applicants then take a test. Those who pass the test are ranked in order. When a position is open, the agency interviews the top three people on the list. One is chosen for the job. This cycle can sometimes take months to complete.

Civil service workers often find themselves working in **bureaucracies**. Sometimes a task as simple as moving a shelf requires filling out forms. Not all government agencies are large and slow to accomplish tasks. However, an impatient person is likely to feel uncomfortable in a government job.

The armed forces also require people with special strengths. Today, the United States has an all-volunteer force. To be accepted, a person must have at least average reading, writing, and thinking skills. People with high school diplomas are preferred. As the number of military personnel becomes smaller, **recruiters** will choose people who show the most promise. Good health is also important. All recruits go through hard physical training and may face extremely tough conditions during wartime.

Military personnel should like following rules and strict routines. They should also like hard work. Above all, they must be committed to protecting and serving the country.

To be accepted into the armed forces, a person must be between 17 and 35 years of age. He or she cannot have been convicted of a felony.

Lifestyle Choices for Government Employees

As you might have guessed, government workers live and work in many different places. Office workers put in eight-hour days five days a week. Police officers and fire fighters work in shifts around the clock. They rarely have weekends off.

Even with budget cuts, government jobs are more secure than jobs in private businesses. Government workers can transfer between agencies. If one job is cut, they have a pretty good chance of finding another. Government workers also have good benefits. For example, full-time workers usually get fully paid medical and dental insurance. The salaries for some positions, such as secretaries, may be higher in private businesses. As a rule, however, government benefits and job security help to offset this difference.

A person who enlists in the armed forces should be prepared for a very different lifestyle. New recruits sign contracts that require them to serve for two to six years. They leave home, family, and friends for several months of training. Once trained, they may serve anywhere in the world. In 1991, the salaries of enlisted personnel started at $697.10 per month. The amount depends on experience, education, and time served. Officers earn more.

Though this monthly salary sounds low, enlisted personnel also have good benefits. They get free room and board and medical and dental benefits. They also get 30 days of vacation per year. Armed forces personnel may also receive training in skills that can be useful in civilian jobs.

Women make up about 11 percent of the armed forces. Today, many of these women train to become mechanics, pilots, and technicians —military careers that were once open only to men.

Careers Practice

Answer these questions on a separate sheet of paper.

1. What are the three steps in getting a civil service job?

2. Should people who want to work near home enlist in the armed forces? Explain.

3. What two health benefits do government workers usually have?

Learn More About It:
The Stay-In-School Program

Ed is a junior in high school. He wants to stay in school, but it will be hard. His mother has just lost her job. His father left the family years ago. His little sisters wear second-hand clothes. Ed wants to help his family. He is thinking about quitting school to work full-time.

Ed goes to his high school counselor and tells him of his plans.

"Hold on," Mr. Johnson says. "We may be able to get you into the Stay-In-School Program."

The Stay-In-School Program provides jobs with the federal government to needy students and to students with **disabilities**. Those who are accepted into the program work part-time while in school. In the summer and during vacation periods, they work full-time. In exchange, the students must stay in school. About 20,000 students participate in the program each year.

To qualify for the Stay-In-School Program, you must be at least 16 years old. You must be disabled or in need of money. You must be working toward a diploma, certificate, or degree. The program is open to students who are in high school, vocational school, or college.

You can find out more about the program in your school office or at your state employment agency. While there, also ask about other programs that help students get work in the federal government.

How to Learn More About Working for the Government

Most libraries are well-stocked with books about government jobs. The *Occupational Outlook Handbook* has a whole section on careers in the armed forces. It is also easy to find government employees who can tell you about working for the government. How easy? Remember that your *teacher* is a government employee!

Here is a little added direction to help you learn about careers in the government.

1. Read federal government job listings. Learn about typical jobs and the education or skills you need to get them. To find these lists, start with your local library. You can also contact one of the 42 Federal Job Information Centers (FJICs). Look under Federal Listings in your phone book to find the FJIC nearest you. You could also go directly to a particular agency. For example, your main post office will carry listings about job openings in the postal service.

2. Also read state and local government job listings. Your state, city, and county employment departments have them. See if you can find at least three careers that interest you.

3. Most libraries carry booklets that help people prepare for civil service exams. Find one for a career you're interested in. Take the practice exams. Doing this can help you pinpoint the skills you must develop before you actually apply.

4. All civil service jobs start with a basic application form. For example, people applying for jobs in the federal government must fill out form SF-171. Obtain such a form and practice filling it out. This will help you learn key words and will show you what information you need to complete the form correctly.

5. If you're considering a career in the military, you can go to a local recruiting office. The recruiter can give you information and discuss your options. To find the nearest recruiting office, look in your phone book or ask at your school office.

6. Those interested in the armed forces can write to the addresses listed below for more information.

Armed Forces Recruiting Information Resources

Department of the Army
HQ US Army Recruiting Command
Fort Sheridan, IL 60037

USAF Recruiting Service
Directorate of Advertising and Publicity
Randolph Air Force Base, TX 78150

Commandant of the Marine Corps
Headquarters
Washington, DC 20380-0001

Navy Recruiting Command
4015 Wilson Blvd.
Arlington, VA 22203-1991

Commandant (G-PRJ)
U.S. Coast Guard
Washington, DC 20590

Chapter Review

Chapter Summary

- The government is the largest employer in the United States. There are about 21 million government workers employed at the federal, state, and local levels.

- There are three groups of government employees. Civil service employees are hired to fill positions. Military personnel enlist in the armed forces. Most government leaders are elected or appointed to their jobs.

- Since the 1980s, the number of government jobs has decreased. This trend is expected to continue.

- People with government jobs should value the missions of the agencies that employ them. Those in the armed forces must be able to follow rules and routines, and to work hard.

- Government jobs and work environments vary greatly. As a rule, the government offers more job security than private industry does. Government workers have good benefits.

- Libraries and government employment agencies carry listings of current job openings. Those interested in the armed forces can talk to local recruiters.

Chapter Quiz

Answer these questions on a separate sheet of paper.

A. Thinking About Careers

1. About how many people are employed by the government?

2. Give an example of a job in state government.

3. Give an example of a job in local government.

4. How does the mayor of your city get his or her job?

5. Are soldiers hired by the armed forces? Explain.

6. What types of personnel cuts are expected in the armed forces by the late 1990s?

7. How have lower taxes affected government employment?

8. What is an important strength needed by all government workers?

9. What hours and days might a police dispatcher work?

10. What is an FJIC? What will you find there?

B. Putting What You Learned to Work

Are your strengths and lifestyle choices suitable to a career in the armed forces? Write a short explanation of why they are or are not.

C. Work Out

What strengths do you think a person must have to run for public office? Describe at least three.

Chapter 15

Working for the Environment

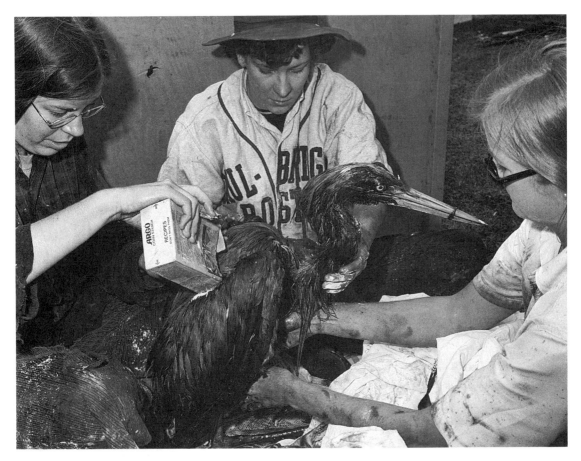

Environmental workers help save and protect wildlife.

Chapter Learning Objectives

- Describe environmental careers.
- Describe trends in environmental careers.
- Match strengths and lifestyle choices to environmental careers.
- List three ways to find out more about environmental careers.

Words to Know

activist   a person who works for change, usually for a social or political cause

conservation   the preservation of natural resources and environments

ecology   the study of how all living things relate to one another and their world

forestry technician   a worker who assists in managing forests

hazardous waste   harmful chemicals or other substances that threaten life

natural resources   resources that are not made by humans, such as air, water, soil, and animals

park technician   a worker who assists in running a park

pollution control technician   a worker who tests water, soil, and air for harmful substances

recycle   to make something able to be used again; to use again

refuse collector   a worker who collects solid waste (garbage) and takes it to a landfill or recycling center

waste management   the industry that cleans waste from the environment and safely stores it

waste water treatment operator   a worker who cleans and treats water from sewers and businesses

wildlife technician   a worker who assists in tracking and caring for animals in a natural setting

---

Ben and Mark walked through the city park together. It was a wonderful day. Birds were singing and children were playing. Ben, however, was not in a good mood.

"I'm so angry with my father," Ben said to Mark. "Today we changed the oil in the car. My dad dumped it out in the backyard even though I told him it could seep through the earth and pollute the ground water. We depend on that for our drinking water. He just laughed. 'What I do or don't do won't make any difference in the world,' he said."

Ben and Mark walked toward the pond. They saw an old woman there picking up litter. She wore a T-shirt that read, "Take Care of Mother Earth."

"Well, I must say, that makes me feel better," Ben laughed. "She believes in making a difference. I do, too, and tomorrow I'm going to join the Environmental Club at school."

"I've heard of that club," Mark said. "What does it do?"

"It's a student-run club that works on community projects. Members teach people about recycling and energy use—things like that—and it's a good way to get experience. I think that after high school I want to work for the environment."

"Great idea," said Mark, "but why wait until tomorrow? We can work for the environment right now."

Ben and Mark joined the woman picking up litter. As they worked, all three were smiling.

Environmental Careers

Ben and Mark are like many people today. They worry about pollution. They worry about the loss of clean air, water, and soil, and about the loss of plant and animal life. They want to make the world a cleaner, safer place. One way people can do this is by choosing environmental careers.

The largest number of environmental careers are in **waste management.** Waste management workers remove the waste from water, soil, and air—even buildings. They try to store the waste where it will not be harmful. **Waste water treatment operators**, for example, operate machines that clean and treat water from sewers and businesses. **Pollution control technicians** test water, air, and soil for harmful chemicals. They also recommend ways to clean up

The United States generates about 10 billion metric tons of waste per year.

polluted areas. **Refuse collectors** pick up garbage from homes and businesses. At one time, most collectors took the garbage to city landfills. Now many also sort garbage so it can be **recycled**.

Many environmental workers are employed in the field of **conservation**. Their mission is to see that our **natural resources** are used wisely and preserved. They work to save water, air, land, plants, and animals for the future. **Wildlife technicians** help manage fish and game for the federal government. Their duties include catching and counting animals. **Forestry technicians** do similar work in the nation's forests. Their main concern, however, is the health of the land and trees. **Park technicians** help park rangers in state and federal parks. They collect fees from park visitors and educate them about caring for the parks. They also see that plants and animals are not destroyed.

Environmental **activists** make up a third group in this field. These activists work to change laws and attitudes about the environment. Some activists are fundraisers. Others help write laws and work to get them passed. The Sierra Club is one of the oldest environmental activist groups in the United States. It has helped pass many laws aimed toward saving the planet's natural resources.

Many environmental activists are unpaid volunteers.

Yellowstone National Park was created in 1872. Thanks to early conservationists, we still enjoy the beauty of this park today.

Trends in Environmental Careers

During the late 1960s and early 1970s, many people began to see the results of pollution. Lake Erie, filled with industrial chemicals, was almost lifeless. Acid rain, also filled with chemicals, fell from the sky. Landfills overflowed with garbage. People began to call for change.

In answer, the federal government passed anti-pollution laws. To enforce them, it created the

Many environmental groups rely on volunteers for fundraising.

The Clean Water Act of 1977 makes it illegal for any industry to discharge any pollutant without a permit.

The Department of Defense is expected to spend nearly $10 billion on cleaning up military bases in the 1990s.

Environmental Protection Agency (EPA). A "Superfund" of $1.6 billion went toward cleaning up **hazardous waste**. In 1986, the Superfund grew to $8 billion.

Hazardous waste, however, turned out to be a larger problem than anyone had imagined. There are still at least 2,000 hazardous waste sites in the United States that need to be cleaned up. Some experts say that there are as many as 10,000 of these sites. This terrible problem does mean jobs. Employment opportunities in waste cleanup and management are expected to increase throughout the 1990s.

It is difficult to judge the job outlook in other environmental fields. Budget cuts have affected employment in state and federal conservation programs. Some states may even close down parks for lack of money. Activists depend more and more on volunteers to keep their organizations growing. Still, workers with good science skills and an interest in the environment should be able to find some jobs in this field.

Careers Practice

Answer these questions on a separate sheet of paper.

1. What does a waste water treatment operator do?

2. What are three examples of natural resources?

3. In what area is job growth expected?

Are Your Strengths Right for an Environmental Career?

People with environmental careers value the earth and its resources. They look toward the future. They want their children and grandchildren to live in beauty, safety, and comfort.

Workers in this field should have a strong interest in science. Math and writing skills are also useful. Environmental technicians must take measurements and keep careful records. Attention to detail is important. Technicians may also have to write reports on their findings. For this reason, good writing skills are helpful. Some careers also require workers with mechanical abilities. For example, waste water treatment operators install, run, and fix equipment in treatment plants.

Environmental activists do not always need strong technical skills. However, having the skills of a good salesperson can be a real plus. After all, their job is to persuade others to believe in their cause. They must also try to convince people to spend their time, money, and voting power on the environment. This is perhaps the toughest job of all.

Lifestyle Choices for Environmental Careers

A career in waste management could take a person just about anywhere. In cities, these workers test buildings and clean up water. Other workers find themselves cleaning up oil spills in the ocean. Still others handle nuclear waste. When around such hazardous waste, workers must wear safety gear and take the utmost care.

People interested in conservation careers are likely to have outdoor jobs. Park, forest, and wildlife technicians usually work in state or federal parks. They can spend days and nights working in the rain or snow. Some climb steep trails to and from work. It is a life for those who truly love the great outdoors. Believe it or not, these jobs are quite competitive. Over 100 applications may come in for just one park ranger opening.

Fundraising jobs are good for those who love the environment but prefer working in an office. However, many activist groups make their money by going door-to-door. Even the fundraiser might get caught in the rain!

Most environmental technicians must have graduated from high school. Classes in biology, physical sciences, math, and **ecology** are important ways to prepare. Many technicians' jobs require at least two years of training in a vocational school or community college. Sometimes, however, a worker is hired out of high school. On-the-job training is then provided.

Have you taken any classes that might help you prepare for an environmental career?

What kind of money can you earn? Beginning park technicians earn between $15,000 and $18,000 per year. The average salary for pollution control technicians was $25,000 in the early 1990s. Paid fundraisers for nonprofit groups typically earn between $15,000 and $20,000 per year.

Careers Practice

Answer these questions on a separate sheet of paper.

1. Why should environmental technicians have good writing skills?

2. What type of environmental worker must have mechanical skills?

3. How long are typical training programs for environmental technicians?

Career Ladder: An Environmental Entrepreneur

When Sheri was 12 years old, her state passed a recycling law. Stores were to refund ten cents for certain cans and bottles. Sheri lived in a neighborhood with careless people. Bottles and cans were left everywhere. She began to gather them daily. Each Saturday, Sheri would cash in the bottles and cans at a nearby store. Week by week, her savings grew.

When Sheri turned 16, she bought a used truck. It wasn't much to look at, but it ran. She began to pick up anything that could be recycled. She found clothing, furniture, books, and more. Second-hand stores paid her cash for many of the things she found.

Now Sheri is using her recycling money to take business classes at a community college.

"I'm thinking about opening my own store," she says. "I'll specialize in selling recycled goods. I like the idea of running my own business while helping the environment. For me, it's the best of both worlds."

How to Learn More About Environmental Careers

There are a number of new books that deal with ways in which people can work for the environment. Look for these resources in your library. Here are some other ideas to help you do your research.

1. Visit organizations or departments in your city that do environmental work. You can try water companies, health departments, recycling centers, and landfills. See what goes on in these places. Talk to the workers about their careers.

2. Do your own environmental project. For example, organize a family project to conserve energy in your home. Get your family's ideas on what to do. Then keep track of your home's gas and electric bills for several months. Later, write a report on whether your project was a success. This will help you develop your skills.

3. Volunteer to work for an environmental organization or for a zoo or local park. These organizations often need help with fundraising and with running various programs. See where your interests lie.

4. Write to vocational schools and community colleges for information on programs in environmental careers.

5. Read job bulletins that list environmental careers. Ask your librarian which bulletins your library carries. If your library doesn't carry any, write to the addresses below. Ask for information on what the resource costs and how to get it.

Environmental Job Listings

Environmental Job Bank
National Wildlife Federation's *Cool It!*
1400 16th Street
Washington, DC 20036

Community Jobs
1520 16th Street NW
Box 147
Washington, DC 20036

Earth Work Magazine
Student Conservation Association
P.O. Box 550
Charlestown, NH 03603

Jobs Bulletin
The Nature People
P.O. Box 98
Warrens, WI 54666

Opportunities
The Natural Science of Youth Foundation
763 Silvermine Road
New Canaan, CT 06840

6. Write to the organizations listed below for more information.

Environmental and Conservation Organizations

American Park Rangers Association
P.O. Box 1348
Homestead, FL 33090

National Environmental Training Association
8687 Via De Ventura
Suite 214
Scottsdale, AZ 85258

North American Association for
   Environmental Education
Bruknew Nature Center
5995 Horseshoe Bend Road
P.O. Box 400
Troy, OH 45373

Student Environmental Action Committee
P.O. Box 1168
Chapel Hill, NC 27514

U.S. Department of Agriculture
Forest Service
P.O. Box 2417
Washington, DC 20013

The Wildlife Society
5410 Grosvenor Lane
Bethesda, MD 20814

Chapter Review

Chapter Summary

- There are many environmental careers. Waste management workers remove waste from water, soil, and air. They also try to store waste safely. Conservationists work to preserve the earth's natural resources and environments. Activists help educate people about environmental problems. They also work to get laws passed.

- The federal government has passed laws and spent billions of dollars to clean up the environment. As a result, many jobs in hazardous waste management have been created. The job outlook in other environmental areas is not as good.

- People who want environmental careers should be interested in science and have math and writing skills. They should be able to keep good records. Some workers in this field must also have mechanical abilities. Environmental activists should be able to persuade others to help their cause.

- Environmental workers may work with hazardous wastes or live healthy lives in the great outdoors. Activists tend to work in offices more. However, they also may spend their time going door-to-door.

- There are many new environmental career resources. Most can be found in libraries. Volunteering and doing environmental projects are good ways to develop skills for environmental careers.

Chapter Quiz

Answer these questions on a separate sheet of paper.

A. Thinking About Careers

1. Give an example of a career in waste management.
2. Give an example of a career in conservation.
3. What do environmental activists do?
4. Give an example of an environmental group that has helped pass many laws.
5. What kind of employment opportunities are expected to increase in the 1990s?
6. Are you likely to have an easy time getting a job as a park ranger? Explain.
7. Why is safety important for workers in waste cleanup?
8. In what environment do wildlife, park, and forest technicians work?
9. Where can high school graduates get training for environmental careers?
10. Where can students volunteer if they are interested in environmental careers?

B. Putting What You Learned to Work

Are your strengths and lifestyle choices suitable to a career working for the environment? Write a short explanation of why they are or are not.

C. Work Out

Greg is a park technician. His summer project is to count the deer in a park. He helps catch and tag them. At the end of the summer, Greg uses his record to help the park ranger write a report on how the deer are doing. Which high school classes could have helped Greg prepare for this job? Explain your answer.

Unit Four Review

Answer these questions on a separate sheet of paper.

1. What does an entrepreneur do?

2. What do entrepreneurs need to start their own businesses?

3. Is the number of parents who work outside the home increasing or decreasing?

4. What skills are taught in parent education classes?

5. Who is the largest employer in the United States?

6. What is the civil service?

7. What is the mission of workers in the armed forces?

8. Where can government job listings be found?

9. What is the mission of people employed in the field of conservation?

10. What do environmental activists do?

Unit Five

Preparing for a Career

Chapter 16

Making a Career Plan

A fast-food job is one possible first step toward becoming a chef.

Chapter Learning Objectives

- Describe four steps that can be used when choosing a career.
- Set a long-term career goal.
- Set short-term career objectives.
- Describe four ways to stay focused on a career plan.

Words to Know

career plan   an outline of what a person wants to achieve; it includes details of how the person wants to achieve the goal; it also includes a time schedule

cons   the reasons *against* doing something

delay   to put off

gratification   a sense of satisfaction or pleasure

objective   a step toward meeting a goal

pros   the reasons *for* doing something

It was Saturday night. John, Liz, Joe, and Karen were sitting in John's living room. They had planned on going out, but they hadn't yet decided where.

"What do you want to do?" Joe asked.

"I don't know. What do you want to do?" Liz replied.

"I don't know," John said.

Karen stood up. "If we keep this up , we won't go anywhere!" she complained. "Let's go see that new movie downtown."

The four young people piled into Karen's car. They enjoyed the film they went to see. Afterwards, they went to a diner.

As John chewed on a french fry, he said, "You know, my mother has been bugging me. She wants to know what I'm going to do after high school. But I don't know. I just can't decide."

"Neither can I," Liz said.

"Same here," said Joe.

Karen put her head in her hands. "Well, I can't help you with this one. If you don't make a career choice, you really won't go anywhere!"

Are you more like Karen or her friends?

Making the Choice

In Chapter 1 of this book, you read why career planning should be important to you. It helps you find work that has meaningful rewards. It saves you time, energy, and money.

In later chapters, you assessed your strengths, made lifestyle choices, and did research. Now it's time to decide on a career. Here are four steps toward doing that.

- *Step 1. Begin with a confident attitude.*

You must trust yourself to be able to make a career choice. Remember that nobody knows you as well as *you* do. Tell yourself, "I *can* do this."

- *Step 2. Match possible careers to your strengths and lifestyle choices.*

Narrow your choices to two or three careers that you think might suit you. Then make a simple chart. At the top, write your career choices. On the left side of the chart, list what you want from a career. Then go down your list. Write an X beside what you will get with each career. Write an O beside what you won't get.

Karen drew up the chart shown below. Notice that neither career gives her *everything* she wants. Both, however, come close.

Karen has listed the pros and cons of each possible career choice.

What I Want	Chef	Banquet Manager
Learn skills on the job in a two-year training program	X	X
Work with food	X	X
Do creative cooking	X	O
Meet many people	O	X
Work in San Francisco	X	X
Work in a first-class hotel or restaurant	X	X
Make at least $18,000 my first year	X	X

- *Step 3. Weigh the* **pros** *and* **cons** *based on your values.*

Karen saw that if she chose to be a chef, her contact with new people would be limited. She would probably see the same kitchen staff every day. For Karen the drawback to being a banquet manager was that she wouldn't be cooking herself. And Karen really enjoyed cooking.

- *Step 4. Make the choice.*

Karen decided that it was more important to her to meet and work with new people. She could always cook at home for her friends. Karen made the choice to become a banquet manager. Once she had made the choice, she was quite happy. She knew that at some point she might have to change her plan. Still, she was glad to have set a direction for herself. When you make your career choice, you will, too.

Careers Practice

Answer these questions on a separate sheet of paper.

1. What is the first step in making a career choice?

2. What is the second step in making a career choice?

3. What is the third step in making a career choice?

Setting a Long-Term Goal

After you've made a career choice, it is time to make a career plan. A **career plan** is an outline of where you want to go and how and when you'll get there.

Begin your career plan by setting a long-term career goal. A career goal is a statement of what you want to achieve by when. Here are three examples of long-term career goals:

- I will be a banquet manager at a large hotel in San Francisco in the next five years.

Make your goal realistic. Set yourself up to succeed, not to fail.

- I will be a radio sportscaster in Miami in six years.
- I will be a self-employed plumber working in my hometown in ten years. My income will be $40,000 per year.

Notice that these goals are stated as "I will be," not "I want to be." Writing the goal in this way will help you keep a positive attitude. Each goal also includes the time by which the goal is to be achieved. Setting a long-term goal for five or ten years from now is a good idea. Long-term goals may also include *where* a person wants to work or *how much* income he or she wants to earn. The more details you include, the easier it will be to know when you've reached your goal. (Remember, too, that you can always change your mind!)

Set Short-Term Career Objectives

When you know *where* you want to go, you then must plan *how* to get there. Do this by setting short-term career objectives.

Career **objectives** are steps that will help you meet your long-term goal. They are ways to gain the skills, knowledge, and experiences your chosen career requires. Like your goal, objectives should be detailed and include target dates.

Here are some examples of short-term career objectives:

- Take a home economics class in my junior year and get an A.
- Volunteer at the nursing home after school for three months this summer.
- Get a part-time job now as a sales clerk in Kimball's Clothing Store to learn sales and cash register skills.

Take a look at Karen's career plan on the next page. As she completes each objective, she'll be one step closer to her long-term goal.

Today's date: September 1, 1995

Long-term career goal: I will be a banquet manager at a large San Francisco hotel in five years.

Objectives	Target Completion Date
1. Take home economics and business math in high school; get Bs or better.	December 1995
2. Apply to food-service management training program in a community college.	January 1996
3. Graduate from high school with a C or better average.	June 1996
4. Get a part-time food-service job in a large hotel in San Francisco.	July 1996
5. Begin food-service management training program.	September 1996
6. Complete food-service management training program.	May 1998
7. Get a job as an assistant banquet manager.	July 1998
8. Apply for banquet manager jobs.	October 2000

Karen's career plan includes a long-term goal and short-term objectives.

Staying Focused

Once you've set your goals and objectives, you're on easy street, right? Not exactly. Following your career plan can be hard work. Here are four things you can do to stay focused.

1. *Write down your career plan and keep it where you can see it.* Post it in your room or inside your locker at school. Look at it every day as a reminder. When you meet an objective, cross it off. Then reward yourself with a pizza, a nap, or some other treat. Remind yourself how good it feels to be moving forward.

2. *Learn to* **delay gratification.** This is a fancy way of saying "put off what you want now in return for future rewards." You might, for example, have to stay home on a Saturday night to study for a test. When your friends are playing ball after school, you might have to work. You know those new shoes you wanted? The money might have to go toward school tuition. You must learn to put off pleasure once in a while. Otherwise, it could be hard to achieve your career goal.

   Don't give up fun altogether, though. Try to lead a balanced and interesting life.

What rewards would help *you* stay on track?

3. *Be flexible.* As you grow and experience new things, your values and strengths will change. As they do, change your career plan—or write a new one. The average person will change careers seven times in his or her lifetime! Without planning, these changes will be more difficult.

4. *See problems as challenges.* It is easy to make excuses when things don't go right. However, excuses won't get you where you want to go. Just think. Beethoven, who was deaf, wrote music. Whoopi Goldberg went from living on welfare to being a Hollywood star. Christy Brown, a writer and artist, had cerebral palsy. The only part of his body that he could move was his left foot. Yet he learned to type and paint with it.

   These people did not make excuses. They met their challenges with courage and drive. When problems arise in *your* life, you should try to do the same.

Take a quiet moment every now and then to think about your career.

Careers Practice

Answer these questions on a separate sheet of paper.

1. What is a career plan?

2. Give an example of a long-term goal.

3. What does it mean to "delay gratification"?

Learn More About It: Accepting Challenge

An 11-year-old boy steps onto the pitcher's mound. It is his first Little League game. The crowd wonders how the boy will pitch. At the end of his right arm is a single large finger. He has no palm with which to grasp the ball. The crowd is afraid the boy will fail.

Young Jim Abbott amazed the fans that day by throwing a no-hitter. He's been amazing fans ever since. Abbott's left arm—his throwing arm—is strong and true. He became a winning pitcher at the University of Michigan with a 26–8 record. In the 1988 Olympics, he pitched a 5–3 victory over Japan to clinch the gold medal. In 1989, the California Angels drafted him into the major leagues. In 1993, he signed a $2 million contract with the New York Yankees.

Jim Abbott doesn't think his success is so amazing.

"Everyone is dealt a problem in life," he says. "Mine is missing four fingers."

Somehow, watching Abbott's 90-mile-an-hour fastball makes it easier to believe that no problem is too large to be overcome.

Chapter Review

Chapter Summary

- Try to begin making a career choice by being confident. List your possible career choices. Weigh what you'll get or give up with each choice. Make your decision based on what you want most.

- A career plan outlines where you want to go. It tells how and when you will get there.

- A long-term goal is a positive statement of the job you want to have and when you want to have it. Most long-term career goals look five to ten years into the future. They can include details such as where a person wants to work or how much the person wants to earn.

- A short-term career objective is a step toward meeting the goal. It includes a date on which the objective will be met.

- Following a career plan can be difficult. To stay on track, write down the plan and keep it where you can see it daily. Cross off objectives after you've met them. Learn to put off pleasurable things for future rewards. Be flexible. Also, see problems as challenges. Rise up to meet and solve them.

Chapter Quiz

Answer these questions on a separate sheet of paper.

A. Thinking About Careers

1. If a person does not make a career choice, what is likely to happen?

2. Who is the best person to choose your career? Why?

3. What role do your values play in making a career choice?

4. What is a career plan?

5. What is a career goal?

6. Give an example of a short-term career objective.

7. What is one way to remind yourself daily of your career plan?

8. Paula decides to study for her college exams rather than go roller blading. What is this an example of?

9. After volunteering at a hospital, Jim learns that he doesn't want to be a nurse. What should he do about his career plan?

10. Name one person who has seen a problem as a challenge and overcome it.

B. Putting What You Learned to Work

Make a chart similar to the one on page 210. List at least two career choices that interest you. Weigh the pros and cons of each. Come to a decision about which is the better of the two.

C. Work Out

Make a career plan. Include a long-term goal and at least three short-term objectives.

Chapter 17

Skill-Building in School

High school is a good time to start preparing for a career. This young person is learning to be on time.

Chapter Learning Objectives
- List two ways in which high school can help a person prepare for a career.
- Tell how to develop a positive attitude.
- Tell how to use time wisely.
- List high school classes that can help build career skills.

Words to Know

attitude a mental outlook
communication the transfer of information from one person or group to another
feedback response from another person about how one has performed

language arts writing, reading, speaking, and other communication skills
negative hopeless or pessimistic
positive hopeful or optimistic
visualize to form a mental picture of; to imagine

Robert sat in history class trying to listen to Mr. Hawthorne talk about the Civil War. Soon, however, Robert's eyes began to close. Then his head fell on the desk with a bang. Startled, he awoke to find the whole class laughing at him.

Mr. Hawthorne said, "Robert, please stay after class. I want to talk to you."

When class ended, an embarrassed Robert stayed behind.

"What's going on with you, Robert?" Mr. Hawthorne asked. "This is the third time this month that you've fallen asleep in class. Are you having trouble at home?"

"No," Robert said. "I took a job after school. I'm helping a friend of my father's add a room to his house. When I get home, I'm too tired to do my homework. Anyway, I figure I learn more on the job than I do at school. I'm learning about building. I'm earning money, too. I don't see what history has to do with my earning a living someday."

Mr. Hawthorne thought for a moment.

"A general comes up with battle plans," he said. "A builder plans houses. In some ways those plans are alike. In some ways, they're different. Think about that. Then let's talk about it some more tomorrow."

That night, Robert read about Civil War battle plans. History began to look a little more meaningful to him.

High School and Your Career

In Chapter 2, you read that high school graduates usually earn more money than people who drop out. They are also less likely to be unemployed. The hope of a better job and a higher income, then, is one very good reason to stay in school.

What do you think is the most important reason to stay in high school?

High school can help you prepare for a career. In school, you can explore and discover your interests and aptitudes. Music, art, writing, debate, sports, and other activities can help you learn more about yourself. This can help you choose a career.

Most importantly, high school is a time to gain knowledge and build skills. Graduating from high school is not a guarantee of getting a job. The job market is competitive. To get a job, a person must be confident and present himself or herself well. Applicants who have good basic math, reading, and writing skills will have a better chance of getting a job than those who do not. School is the time to build those skills. In high school, you can train for a career, the way that an athlete prepares for a sports event. This training begins with attitude.

The Importance of Attitude

Attitude is a mindset or mental outlook. It is a way of looking at things. Before his talk with Mr. Hawthorne, Robert saw history as useless. With Mr. Hawthorne's help, Robert's outlook started to change. He began to look for ways in which history could be meaningful to him and his work. Robert found that having a **positive** attitude made studying easier.

People with positive attitudes are cheerful and

energetic. They look for the good side in what happens. People with **negative** attitudes are moody, angry, or sad. Nothing is ever quite right. They sometimes feel that the world is out to get them.

Employers tend to hire workers with positive attitudes. Positive people enjoy their work. Their co-workers find them easy to be around. They also tend to be good problem-solvers. Their attitude helps them see problems as opportunities rather than as reasons to give up.

Who do you know that has a positive attitude?

Getting and keeping a positive attitude is a skill. Developing a positive attitude in high school will do more than help you prepare for a career. It will also help you enjoy high school!

Here are some things you can do to develop and maintain a positive attitude:

- Before you go to sleep at night, focus on one positive event in the day. It could be something you learned, a good time you had with a friend, a smile someone gave you. Make this the last thing you think about before falling asleep.
- When you wake up in the morning, **visualize** the good things that will happen to you. See yourself learning and having fun.
- Think of how school will help you prepare for the future.
- Here is a real challenge. Make a habit of looking for the positive side of not-so-positive events. Tim, for example, got an F on a test that he had studied hard for. At first, he felt terrible. He never wanted to study again. Then he spoke with his teacher.

  "I'm just not getting this on my own," he said. "I need extra help. Can you give it to me?"

  Tim's teacher found a tutor for him. In time, his grades improved in every subject. Now he looks back at getting the F as having been the start of something positive.

- Reflect your positive attitude in how you look and act. Stand tall and smile. Be friendly and helpful. Have a sense of humor when things look glum. Others will begin to appreciate your positive attitude and look to you for help. You may find yourself becoming a role model.

Using Time Wisely

Shane is always late for class. He leaves his homework until the last minute and then rushes through it. His sister Sarah is just the opposite. She's always on time. Her assignments are well planned and clearly thought out.

Imagine that you are an employer. Both Shane and Sarah come to you asking for a job. You know their school habits. Which one are you more likely to hire?

You will probably hire Sarah. Employers want workers who have good attendance, who are on time, and who get their work done. They want people who can use their time wisely.

How do you develop this skill? A good way to begin is to record how you use your time right now. Keep a diary of what you do on a school day. You could find that you spend four hours in front of the TV. Or you might be spending two hours on the phone. Another hour might be spent listening to music.

Next, set your goals and objectives for school. Your goal could be to pass all your classes this year with a C or better. Your objectives could be:

- Have perfect attendance (unless really sick).
- Be on time for every class.
- Complete homework each day.

When you know your objectives, you can use your time to meet them. Shane, for example, found that he spent 20 minutes in the shower every morning. And every morning he was late for his first class. Shane decided to cut down his time in the shower to ten minutes. The extra ten minutes he got from changing his routine enabled him to get to class on time.

How else might Shane have changed his routine to get to class on time?

More Time-Use Tips

1. Set aside at least two hours for homework at the same time each day. Let your family and friends know that this time is for homework only.

2. Break large homework assignments into smaller tasks. Schedule these tasks into your homework time each day.

3. Reward yourself after you've done your homework. Use this time to do something you like.

4. Keep track of your attendance.

Careers Practice

Answer these questions on a separate sheet of paper.

1. Is graduating from high school a guarantee of getting a job? Explain.

2. What is attitude?

3. John is late for his fourth-period class every day. Fourth period is right after lunch. When John looks at how he uses his time, he discovers why. It takes him 20 minutes to walk to a restaurant he likes. He spends 30 minutes eating. Then it takes him 20 minutes to walk back. His lunch period is only 50 minutes long. What could John do differently to be on time for class?

Building Communication Skills

"Wanted: person with good communication skills. Must be able to follow written directions. Good speaking skills a must."

Think about a career that interests you. What communication skills would you need to do that job well?

These phrases are often found in want ads and job listings. Just about every employer wants workers who have good communication skills. **Communication** is the transfer of information from one person or group to another. A stock clerk communicates when she writes down the number of items in a warehouse. A salesperson communicates with customers when he tells them about a product. A road-crew worker communicates when she signals to cars with her hands.

High school English and **language arts** classes are good places to build communication skills. Writing classes teach you how to organize and communicate information on paper or on a computer. Reading classes teach you how to understand and apply written information. Speech classes teach you how to present information aloud in an understandable, entertaining way. Building your communication skills doesn't just happen in English classes, however. You are practicing communication skills every time you listen, take notes, write letters, or read.

Many schools offer fun ways to build communication skills. Students on debate teams learn to persuade. Students on school newspapers write stories about events that are important to young people. In school plays, student actors learn to entertain. Taking part in these activities is a good way to learn how to give and receive information.

Does your school offer a computer class? If so, add taking the class to your list of career objectives.

Many of today's jobs require workers to put information into computers. If your high school has computers, it is a good idea to learn to use them. Practice using a computer as much as possible. Write papers on it. Schedule your day on it. Keep track of important events on it. Computer skills can look very good to possible employers. Someday, they may be just what you need to get a good job.

Building Math Skills

Like communication skills, math skills are needed on just about every job. A nurse's aid counts a pulse for ten seconds and multiplies it by six to determine a patient's heartbeats per minute. A drywall installer figures the square footage of a room to decide how much of each building material to buy. A salesperson keeps track of the miles she drives each month and figures out how much gas money her company owes her. Workers also need math skills to check the amounts on their paychecks and to figure their taxes.

Most high schools require students to take at least a basic math class. These classes teach students how to add, subtract, multiply, and divide. They may also provide practice in using calculators and computers to do math.

If you're thinking about a career in technology, advanced math classes will be helpful. Skills learned in algebra and geometry can be used by builders, computer programmers, and even health workers. Some high schools offer classes in business math. Business math is especially helpful for those who want sales careers or careers working in offices. Would-be entrepreneurs will also find it helpful.

You do not have to be a math wizard to get a good job. However, you do need the basic skills. High school offers the best opportunity to get them.

Classes and Activities for Chosen Careers

Marty wants to be a nurse. She takes health and biology classes. She puts extra effort into getting good grades in these subjects. Pedro wants to be mayor of the city someday. He takes history and government classes. He also runs for student office. Tanya wants to be a graphic artist. She takes art classes and helps design posters for school events.

As you saw in Units Three and Four, career research includes learning how to prepare for a career. Certain high school classes will prepare you for your chosen career more than others will. Your school counselor can direct you to those that are the most useful. However, it is up to you to do well in them.

Careers Practice

Answer these questions on a separate sheet of paper.

1. Give an example of how a sales clerk might communicate on the job.

2. What classes focus on building communication skills?

3. Why should everyone who earns a paycheck have basic math skills?

Learning to take others' advice is a useful skill. It comes in handy both in school and on the job.

Learn More About It: Using Feedback

Theresa didn't like her English class at all. Every paper she turned in came back marked up with red ink. When she saw the red marks, she felt ashamed and angry. Often she tore up such papers. To her, the marks said, "You're no good. You failed."

When Theresa brought home a D in English, her father sat down with her.

"It's that red ink," Theresa explained. "The marks are all over my paper. The teacher wants everything perfect. I just make so many mistakes!"

"Start bringing the papers home instead of tearing them up," her father said. "We'll look at them together."

Theresa did this. Her father helped her figure out what the red marks meant. Theresa had made many of the same mistakes again and again. Her father showed her how to correct them. Soon her papers were coming back with fewer red marks on them. In time, a paper with a perfect score was returned. That night, Theresa and her father went out to celebrate.

"Learning to use **feedback** is an important skill," Theresa's father said to her over dinner. "Our teachers and bosses don't always respond to our work in the most helpful ways. Still, it's up to us to take the feedback and improve ourselves."

Theresa agreed. Later, when she became a teacher, she taught her students how to use the feedback she gave them. However, she never used red ink to mark her students' papers!

Chapter Review

Chapter Summary

- Graduating from high school doesn't guarantee a job. To prepare for careers, students should use high school to discover their interests and aptitudes. High school is also a means of gaining knowledge and developing important career skills.

- A positive attitude is helpful both in getting hired and in completing school. Getting and keeping a positive attitude is a skill. Work on a positive attitude by focusing on successes and seeing the good side of things.

- Employers like workers who use their time well. Learning how to use time well can also help students complete their schooling. To learn to use time well, keep track of how you use time now. Then set objectives for what you want to achieve in school. Change the way you use your time to meet those objectives.

- Communication skills are needed on almost every job. English and language arts classes help build reading, writing, and speaking skills. School activities such as acting, debating, and writing for the school paper can also be helpful.

- Workers need at least basic math skills. High schools offer classes that teach students to add, subtract, multiply, and divide. Students who want technical careers should also take more advanced math classes, such as algebra and geometry. Business math is also helpful for many careers.

- Particular classes can help students prepare for particular careers. By doing career research, a person can find out which classes are the most important to take and do well in.

- The feedback we get from the work we do may not always please us. Usually, however, we can learn from it.

Chapter Quiz

Answer these questions on a separate sheet of paper.

A. Thinking About Careers

1. Who is likely to earn more money—high school graduates or those who do not finish high school?
2. What is one way high school can help a person prepare for a career?
3. What is a positive attitude?
4. What is one way to get and keep a positive attitude?
5. Why do employers want workers who know how to use their time well?
6. What is the first step in changing how you use your time?
7. What communication skills are learned in writing classes?
8. What are some school activities other than classes that can help build communication skills?
9. Who could be helped by taking a business math class?
10. What is another word for "feedback"?

B. Putting What You Learned to Work

Which skill do you think you most need to develop? Write a short plan of what you could do to build this skill in high school.

C. Work Out

Keep a record of how you spend your time over a three-day period. Write down each activity and the amount of time you spend doing it. For example: "Watched TV from 3:30 to 5:30." Are you using your time as well as you can to meet your goals and objectives? If not, explain what you could change.

Chapter 18

More Ways to Get Experience

First jobs may not be glamorous, but they're a good way to get experience.

Chapter Learning Objectives

- List four ways to get experience.
- Describe how internships work.
- Describe how mentoring programs work.
- Describe how to find volunteer opportunities.

Words to Know

internship   an on-the-job learning and training program

mentor   an experienced person who helps and advises an inexperienced person

protégé   a person who is guided or helped by a more experienced person

recommendation   a written or spoken statement that someone or something is worthwhile or valuable

tutoring   one-to-one teaching

Penny and Ty had gone out looking for summer work. They filled out applications at a nearby ice cream store. They applied at a fast-food restaurant. They put up posters saying they were available for yard work and babysitting.

At the end of the day, they sat and talked over lemonade.

"I don't know why I'm doing this," Ty said. "My chances of getting a job are slim. Even if I do get hired, the job will be a dead-end one. Scooping ice cream doesn't have anything to do with my career plans."

"Oh?" said Penny. "What are you planning to do?"

"I want to become an auto mechanic," Ty said. "I tried to get work in an auto shop, but nobody's hiring kids this summer."

"Well," Penny said, "even an auto mechanic has to know how to talk to different kinds of people."

"Yes, but so what?" Ty answered.

"You would also have to add up bills and take payments, right?"

"I guess so," Ty replied.

"Well, you'd be doing the same thing on one of these 'dead end' jobs, wouldn't you?"

Ty slapped Penny on the back. "You got me there," he said. "I suppose almost any job is a way to get experience."

Suddenly, Penny stopped smiling. "But what if we don't get jobs—*any* jobs? How will we get experience then?"

Ty shrugged. A job at the ice cream store was looking better and better all the time.

Ways to Get Experience

If you've ever applied for work, you've been asked, "What experience do you have?" Employers like to hire people with experience for several reasons. If a worker already has a certain skill, such as running a computer, the employer saves time and money training that person.

Employers also feel that it is less risky to hire someone with experience. Quite often, employers call a person's past employers for **recommendations**. A good recommendation lets the employer know that a worker has done well in the past. The worker is therefore more likely to do well in the future.

Most young people find it hard to get experience. "How can I get experience if no one will hire me?" they say. Like Penny and Ty, you can sometimes get jobs that do not require any experience. "First jobs" include babysitting, delivering newspapers, and working at fast-food restaurants. These are good jobs to have while you're still in school. They help you develop skills, gain experience, and earn a bit of money. Your employers can give you recommendations for later jobs, too.

Even first jobs can be tough to get, though. However, there are at least three other ways for a young person to get experience:

- Internships

Unit Six of this book includes information on applying for jobs.

- Mentoring programs
- Volunteer positions

Internships

Heather is an intern at a local radio station. She spends two hours a day after school working there. She has many duties, including taking calls and answering mail from listeners. In exchange, she learns how the station operates. She also meets people who have careers in radio. She hopes that these contacts will someday help her find a job. In three months, Heather's internship will end. It will have been an important experience—one that she can put on her job applications.

An **internship** is an on-the-job learning and training experience. Internships are usually offered by businesses that want to provide opportunities for young people. Some interns work on newspapers, in large computer companies, and in factories. The work can be part-time or full-time, paid or unpaid. Internships might last a summer or up to a year. Sometimes they are done for class credit. Companies who hire interns expect them to work hard. In exchange, interns gain experience and develop job skills.

Finding and getting an internship takes planning and work. A good way to begin is to ask your high school counselor. Your local librarian might also have ideas. Community employment agencies may have internship listings as well.

To get an internship, you will have to apply for it, much as you apply for a job. Many internships require that you apply at least six months before the work is to begin. The application will ask why you want the internship. Be prepared to explain that the internship is one objective in your career plan. The more serious you are, the more seriously you will be considered.

Is there a company that you would really like to work for? Call that company's employment department and ask if it offers internships.

A good resource for internships is the *Washington D.C. Internship Directory.* It is published yearly by the Congressional Youth Leadership Council. This book focuses mainly on government internships in the Washington D.C. area. Many of these internships are for college students or adults. However, the book contains many good tips on how to apply for and get internships. Any person applying for an internship will find it a useful resource.

Mentoring Programs

Mentoring programs are different from internships. In a mentoring program, an experienced person is paired with a less experienced person. The experienced person—the **mentor**—becomes a source of support for his or her **protégé**. The mentor may provide advice, job contacts, **tutoring**, or a shoulder to cry on. The mentor and protégé decide on activities that suit their strengths and needs.

Mentors lend support, knowledge, and experience to young people.

Mentoring programs are becoming quite popular today. Two of the best-known mentoring programs are Big Brothers and Big Sisters. In these programs, an adult works with a young person to provide support. The Big Sister or Big Brother also acts as a role model for the younger person.

The Black Achievers Program is found in more than 40 YMCAs around the country. Its purpose is to help inner-city youth from grades 7 to 12 finish school. The Black Achiever mentors also help their protégés get job experience.

In Project Primer, a program in Oakland, California, African American and Latino high school students act as mentors. They work with elementary school students. They tutor, teach values, and act as role models. The mentors in this program benefit from giving of themselves. They feel good because they're helping people. They are also getting important experience in learning how to teach.

You may want to join a mentoring program either as a mentor or a protégé. If you join as a protégé, decide what you want from your mentor before you join. Be aware that having a mentor is not the same as having a fairy godmother. The mentor provides experience and support. It is up to the protégé to work hard and use this support in a responsible way.

If you become a mentor, make sure you join a program that provides mentor training. Being a mentor takes important skills. Mentors must know how to listen well, to give support and advice, and to help their protégés achieve. In most cases, mentors are not paid.

Would you make a good mentor?

Careers Practice

Answer these questions on a separate sheet of paper.

1. What is an internship?

2. What might a mentor do?

3. What is a protégé?

Volunteering

Throughout this book, you have read that volunteering is a good way to get experience. Volunteers are unpaid workers. They are welcome and needed in many non-profit organizations. Hospitals, clinics, schools, churches, and homeless shelters are just a few places that use volunteers.

Volunteering is not for everyone. Before you volunteer, ask yourself these questions:

- Am I willing to give my time and energy without being paid?
- Am I flexible?
- Can I work independently?
- Can I work with people who are different from me?

If you answer "yes," volunteering could be a good way for you to get experience.

How do you find a place to volunteer? Begin by reviewing your career plan. If you're thinking of a health career, perhaps nursing home patients in your area could use your care. Projects that develop community housing offer possibilities to those interested in the trades. A future salesperson might spend time raising money for a food bank or an environmental group.

Decide how much time you want to spend volunteering and when. Use your time in such a way that volunteering does not get in the way of your

Volunteers can get experience in different career fields. These young people are learning about environmental careers by volunteering in a paper recycling project.

schooling. Once a week for several hours might be a good amount of time. In the summer, you may want to volunteer more often.

In the front of many phone books are sections called "Community Services Numbers." The services listed there often need volunteers. Churches, synagogues, fire departments, libraries, nursing homes, police stations, and schools are using more and more volunteers these days.

Do some research on any organization that interests you. Try to pick one that will serve *your* needs at the same time that you're serving its needs. Talking to

Look at your career plan. Where could you volunteer to get the experience you need?

former volunteers is a good way to get information. They can tell you what their experiences were like. They may also provide tips on making your own experience worthwhile.

The next step is to call the organizations that interest you. Explain that you want to be a volunteer. Be clear about the kind of work you want to do and the time you can offer. If an organization can use you, ask about volunteer training. First-time volunteers should get training in how to perform their jobs. Otherwise, they may feel frustrated and helpless. Good organizations will prepare their volunteers to do good jobs.

For more information about where and how to volunteer, write to:

Volunteers of America National Headquarters
3813 North Causeway Boulevard
Metairie, LA 70002

Careers Practice

Answer these questions on a separate sheet of paper.

1. Do all people make good volunteers? Explain.

2. What is one way to find an organization that needs volunteers?

3. Why would you ask a volunteer organization if it offers training?

Learn More About It: School-to-Work

The year: 2001. The place: Central High School, Anywhere, USA. At least half the juniors and seniors are enrolled in apprenticeship programs. They train as metal workers, machinists, and electronics technicians. They will leave school with certificates in job specialties. Most will be hired by the companies that trained them. Unemployment is at an all-time low for young people.

Is this science fiction? Not to the students in the six "school-to-work" transition programs that are already in place. The purpose of these programs is to train young people who are not college-bound for future jobs. The students begin apprenticeships while still in high school or community college. As part of the apprenticeships, they work part-time for businesses. The schools provide classroom training. Upon graduation, students are certified in their chosen fields. These school-to-work programs prepare young people for careers in health, banking, and more.

The idea of school-to-work programs is catching on. In 1991, Oregon and Wisconsin passed laws that will help create such programs on a statewide basis. The federal government and private organizations have spent $10 million toward helping these programs succeed.

For more information on school-to-work programs in your area, contact these organizations:

Jobs For the Future
1815 Massachusetts Ave.
Cambridge, MA 02140

Office of Work-Based
   Learning
Employment and Training
   Administration
U.S. Labor Department
200 Constitution Ave., N.W.
Washington, DC 20210

In Germany, about half the young people between the ages of 15 and 18 are in apprenticeship programs.

Chapter Review

Chapter Summary

- Employers like to hire workers who have experience. Experienced workers save employers time and money in training. Also, employers feel that it is less risky to hire experienced workers.

- To get experience, young people can apply for "first jobs." Babysitting, delivering newspapers, and fast-food jobs usually do not require experience. Internships, mentoring programs, and volunteer programs are other ways to get experience.

- Internships are on-the-job learning and training experiences.

- Mentoring programs match experienced mentors with inexperienced protégés. The mentors help their protégés by giving support, advice, and opportunities.

- Volunteers are unpaid workers. Most volunteer opportunities are available in non-profit organizations. Before volunteering, a person should be clear about the kind of experience he or she wants. First-time volunteers should seek organizations that provide training.

Chapter Quiz

Answer these questions on a separate sheet of paper.

A. Thinking About Careers

1. List three "first jobs" that do not usually require a person to have experience.

2. What is one reason why employers like to hire experienced workers?

3. How do employers check to see if a job applicant was a good worker in past jobs?

4. What is an internship?

5. Are internships paid or unpaid?

6. What is a mentoring program?

7. What type of organization uses many volunteers?

8. What are three places to look for volunteer opportunities?

9. Why is it a good idea for first-time volunteers to have training?

10. How can you learn whether or not an organization is a good place to volunteer?

B. Putting What You Learned to Work

Which would help you most with your long-term career goal—an internship, mentoring, or a volunteer program? Explain why.

C. Work Out

If you had a mentor, how would you want that person to support you? Think back to your career plan and objectives. Where could you use the most help?

Unit Five Review

Answer these questions on a separate sheet of paper.

1. What is a career plan?

2. What are career objectives?

3. What should you do with your career plan as your values and strengths change?

4. What is one way to stay focused on achieving a career plan?

5. Why do employers like to hire workers with positive attitudes?

6. What classes teach communication skills?

7. Why do all workers need at least basic math skills?

8. Why do employers like to hire experienced workers?

9. What are three programs that provide experience for young people?

10. What are three ways to find volunteer opportunities?

Getting a Job

Chapter 19

Searching for Jobs

Hunting for job prospects is hard work. The more methods you use, the more likely you are to find a job.

Chapter Learning Objectives

- Describe four ways to make a job search more effective.
- Tell how to find job prospects by networking.
- Tell how to find job prospects through published resources.
- Tell how to find job prospects through employment offices.

Words to Know

abbreviation   a shortened form of a word

acquaintance   a person known slightly, not someone who is a good friend or a relative

directory   a published resource that lists information for a certain area or subject

network   a system of connected lines that transmits information

prospect   a future possibility or chance

rejection   a refusal; a turndown

temporary   lasting for a short time

trade magazine   a magazine that contains articles and information about a particular industry

---

It was a beautiful Saturday morning. Mario had called his friend Leo to find out if he wanted to play ball.

"No," Leo said. "I received some bad news yesterday. I was laid off from my job."

"That's too bad," Mario said. "You must feel awful. Are you sure you don't want to play ball? It might help you feel better."

"Well, I know that feeling awful won't get me a job. But neither will playing ball. I'm looking at the want ads right now. I'll talk to you later."

Two weeks went by. Mario called Leo again and invited him to a movie.

"I can't," Leo said. "I'm going to a job fair tonight."

"Oh, right," Mario said. "Maybe next week."

Three weeks later, Mario called Leo again. "Hey, buddy, how about going out tonight?" he asked.

"No thanks. I have a job interview in the morning," Leo said. "I need to be well rested for it."

Mario felt put off. "Aren't you spending a little too much time on this job-searching?" he asked. "What about spending some time with your friends?"

"You're right," Leo said. "Let's get together soon. I've been meaning to ask you if you have any job leads. I'd like to tell you exactly what I'm looking for."

Mario shook his head. "You just don't give up, do you?"

The Job Search

Leo is a dedicated job seeker. He knows that finding job **prospects** is hard work. It takes time, energy, and willpower. Career experts have come up with several ways to make the job search more effective. Here are four of the most important ones:

1. Always review your career research and career plan before searching for a job. Remember why you want a job and which jobs will best match your strengths and desires. Review your lifestyle choices as well. Think about the work environment that most appeals to you. Decide whether you want part-time, full-time, or temporary work. Aim for a realistic starting income. A rewarding career is one that suits you. What do you most want to do? Keep your goal in mind at all times!

2. Be realistic about how long it takes to find a job. Surveys show that the average time it takes to get a job is between 8 and 23 weeks. Sometimes it takes even longer. If you start out knowing this, you are less likely to become discouraged. There is one possible way to shorten the overall search length, however. Most job seekers spend only about five hours a week searching for jobs. The more hours you spend looking for work, the sooner you are likely to find it.

3. The more methods you use, the more likely you are to be successful. If, for example, you look in the want ads *and* ask friends about job openings, you're

Career expert Richard Nelson Bolles recommends spending 20 hours per week on the job search.

more likely to find a job than someone who only looks in the want ads. Keep this in mind when searching for job prospects. Make use of every opportunity.

4. Get support from family and friends during your job search. Join a group of job seekers who know what it's like to search for work. All people go through ups and downs during the job search. Their hopes rise and fall with each application and **rejection.** Supportive people can help keep each other from giving up.

One out of every three job hunters gives up looking for a job because it takes so long.

How to Network

There are many ways to search for jobs. One of the most effective is to network. A **network** is a system of interconnected lines that transmits information. When you network, you build a system of people who can receive and pass along job information for you. For example, Leo talked to his friend Mario about the kind of job he wanted. Mario didn't know of any jobs, but he passed along the information to his boss. His boss had a friend who was looking for workers. This information went back through the network to Mario, who then arranged for a job interview.

How do you go about networking? The first step is to make a list of all the people you want to inform that you're looking for work. Begin by returning to the career research you already did. Look at the people you did informational interviews with. Did they tell you about any companies that might hire you? Did they give you the names of any other people you might contact? If not, call the people again. Tell them you are ready to look for work. Ask if they have any job leads for you.

Now add family members to your list. That includes aunts, uncles, and distant cousins whom you haven't seen for years. Next, write down the friends and **acquaintances** who might be able to provide you with job leads. In this group, include teachers, counselors, neighborhood store owners, old boyfriends and girlfriends—everyone!

The next step is to contact the people on your list. When you call, explain who you are and why you're calling. Tell what job you're looking for. If the people you speak to have any leads, write them down. Also, ask them to pass on what you have told them if they hear of any possibilities. Ask them to get back in touch with you if they hear of anything.

Let people know how to reach you. Sometimes it helps to pass out cards with your name and phone number on them. (In Chapter 20, you'll learn about writing a résumé. Passing out your résumé can also be helpful when you're networking.) Make it easy for people to contact you. Be polite and say thank you.

In time, your networking efforts will pay off.

Networking is an effective way of finding job leads.

Careers Practice

Answer these questions on a separate sheet of paper.

1. How long do most job searches take?

2. How can a support group help in a job search?

3. In a job search, what does it mean to network?

Using Published Resources

A number of published resources can also be used to find job prospects. John, for example, wanted to be a writer. He went to his local library and found a book called *Jobs for Writers*. It described writing careers and places to apply. He also found a book called *Job Hunting in the Seattle Area*. In this resource, he was able to find job leads in the area where he lived.

Libraries usually have **directories** that can be useful in job-hunting, too. There are directories that list professional groups, trade schools, and employment resources. Such directories could also provide contacts for your networking list. Ask the librarian if you need help finding directories for the career you want.

Another printed resource used by job seekers is the want ads. Want ads appear in newspapers and **trade magazines.** The ads include short summaries of the skills and experience the employers want. Sometimes the ads include information about income and hours as well. Want ads also tell you how and where to apply for the jobs.

Want ads are usually listed in alphabetical order by job title or job area. For example, a person looking for a teacher's aid job could look under Education or under Teachers.

Under what headings in the wants ads could you find listings for your long-term career goals?

When applying for jobs in the want ads, be aware that thousands of job seekers are reading the same newspaper you are. This means that hundreds—even thousands!—of people may answer the same ad that you do. Answering ads can still be worthwhile, however. Job seekers who use this method should simply be ready for a lot of competition. They should use other methods of job-searching as well.

You should also be aware that many job openings are not announced in the want ads.

Where can you find bulletin boards in your community?

Another way to find work is through want ads on bulletin boards. With this method you are more likely to find **temporary** part-time work than permanent full-time work. A typical bulletin board could carry ads for babysitters, gardeners, laborers, and housekeepers. Workers can advertise themselves on bulletin boards, too. If you post such a notice, include the type of work you can do, the hours you're available, and your phone number. A date on the notice is also helpful. Where do you find bulletin boards? Libraries, schools, markets, and laundromats often have them. Look around for one in your community and make a practice of reading it.

Using Employment Offices

Many job seekers use employment offices when searching for job prospects. Employment offices have lists of job openings. They usually have employment specialists who help match workers and jobs.

Colleges, trade schools, and sometimes high schools have employment offices. They operate free of charge. As a rule, only people who have attended the school can use the employment service. These offices work hard at placing former students in jobs. Whenever a student is placed, it helps the school show that it can successfully prepare students for careers. This helps the school attract new students.

Learn More About It:
Interpreting the Want Ads

To save space, newspaper want ads use many **abbreviations,** or shortened forms of words. This list will help you understand what common abbreviations mean.

Abbreviation	Meaning
adm. asst.	administrative assistant (office job similar to a secretary position)
appt.	appointment
B.A./B.S.	Bachelor of Arts/Bachelor of Science (four-year college degree)
co.	company
emp. agy.	employment agency
EOE	Equal Opportunity Employer
exc. opty.	excellent opportunity
exp'd	experienced
exp. nec.	experience necessary
exp. pref.	experience preferred
exp. req.	experience required
F/T	full-time
mgr.	manager
NS	non-smoker
perm.	permanent
P/T	part-time
refs	references
sal. reqs.	salary requirements
temp.	temporary
W/P	word processing
wpm	words per minute
$10K–$12K	$10,000 to $12,000 per year

For this reason, using school offices is a good method of finding work.

Another free service is offered by the United States Employment Service (USES). This employment service has offices in every state. Your state office might be called the Employment Development Department, Job Service, or State Employment Office. Because of recent budget cuts, state offices are usually understaffed. However, they are still good places to learn about job openings. To find the office in your area, look in the state listings in the front of your phone book.

There are also private employment agencies. These charge fees to help people find jobs. Sometimes the fee is paid by the employer, sometimes by the employee. Such agencies usually specialize in handling certain job areas. For example, many agencies find temporary positions for office workers.

Before using a private agency, look into it carefully. Ask about fees and job specialties. Ask about the agency's success rate in finding jobs for people. If possible, talk to another person who has used the service. Find out what he or she liked or didn't like about it.

Careers Practice

Answer these questions on a separate sheet of paper.

1. What are two places to look for want ads?

2. What is one drawback to finding jobs in the want ads?

3. What does USES stand for?

Chapter Review

Chapter Summary

- Searching for a job takes time, energy, and willpower. To make the job search easier, keep your career goals and objectives in mind. Be prepared to spend 8 to 23 weeks, or even longer, on your job search. Use as many job-seeking methods as possible to increase your chances of getting a job. Join a support group while you're searching.

- Networking is a good way to collect job information. Tell friends, family, and acquaintances about your job search. Ask them if they can give you any leads. Ask the people you did informational interviews with for job leads.

- There are many published resources that can provide job leads. Books and directories can help job seekers find leads in certain careers. Want ads in newspapers and trade magazines, as well as notices on bulletin boards, can also be helpful. Want ads can be placed by employers or workers. Employers often get hundreds of responses to want ads.

- Employment agencies try to match workers with jobs. School placement offices and state employment offices provide this service for free. Private employment agencies charge fees. They are paid by either the employer or the employee.

Chapter Quiz

Answer these questions on a separate sheet of paper.

A. Thinking About Careers

1. On average, how long does it take to find a job?

2. What is one way to shorten the overall time it takes to find a job?

3. How many methods should you use to find work? Why?

4. What is one thing that people in a support group can help do for each other?

5. When a job seeker is networking, what is he or she doing?

6. When networking, what should a job seeker tell people?

7. Why should job hunters use more than just the want ads to find job prospects?

8. What are four kinds of jobs that might be found on a bulletin board?

9. Who can use school employment offices?

10. How would you find the state employment office in your area?

B. Putting What You Learned to Work

Make a list of at least ten people whom you could tell about your job search. Write a short paragraph about what you would say to them when you network.

C. Work Out

Job seekers sometimes place "Work Wanted" ads in newspapers. Write an ad for a job you would like to have. Keep the ad under 30 words in length. Include your skills and experience, as well as your income and time requirements.

Chapter 20

Applying for Jobs

Applying for a job in person increases your chances of being hired.

Chapter Learning Objectives

- List three ways to apply for jobs effectively.
- Fill out a job application.
- Write a résumé.
- Write a cover letter.

Words to Know

action verbs words that show action, such as "run," "plan," or "direct"

candidate a person seeking a position

cover letter a short letter to an employer that is included with a job application or résumé

human resources department a department that screens job applicants and administers employee records and benefits; called the *personnel department* in some companies

proofread to carefully read a written piece and mark any corrections needed

résumé a written statement of a worker's experience, education, and personal information

social security number a number issued by the federal government for tax purposes

Cathy and Maya had just finished track practice. The young women decided to jog home from school and clean up there. They ran at an easy pace toward their neighborhood. Suddenly, Cathy stopped.

"Look," she said to Maya. "There's a sign in that new clothing store. It says, 'Part-time work available. Apply within.' "

"So?" Maya replied.

"So I've been looking for part-time work. Plus I love the clothes in that store. You know I want to be a fashion designer someday. Let's go in, and I'll apply."

Maya laughed. "Girl, are you crazy? Look at yourself." She turned Cathy around so that she could see her reflection in the store's window. Both young women were dressed in their jogging clothes. They were dripping with sweat, and their hair was blown every which way.

Now Cathy started to laugh. "You're right. I guess this isn't the right moment to apply."

Applying for Jobs

Like Cathy, someday you may find a job that seems perfect to you. Like Cathy, your first impulse could be to ask for the job as quickly as you can. Such enthusiasm is fine, unless—like Cathy—you are unprepared. Most employers require job seekers to fill out applications or supply résumés, or do both. Applications and résumés provide employers with information about work experience and skills.

Employers often hear from dozens of job seekers. Well-prepared applications and résumés can lead to job interviews. Then the best **candidate** is selected. However, small mistakes can land a résumé or job application in the wastebasket. It's worth your time to make yours as good as you can make it.

Experts say that 47 out of 100 job seekers who apply in person get the jobs they want.

How else can you increase your chances of getting through the application process to the interview? When possible, apply in person. If possible, contact the person who is doing the hiring. In small companies, this will usually be the manager or the owner. In large businesses and government organizations, you may have to go through the **human resources** (personnel) **department** or the employment office.

When you apply in person, look your best. Dress neatly in clean clothing that is appropriate to the work you would be doing. Smile, shake hands, be friendly. Give the person a reason to remember you in a positive way. If Cathy had applied at the clothing store in her jogging clothes, the store manager would have remembered her as eager but sloppy. The manager would not have been impressed.

It isn't always possible or practical to apply in person. Sometimes you'll have to mail in an application or a résumé. In that case, make sure that you mail in your papers on time.

Whether you apply in person or by mail, supply the best-looking, most complete application or résumé that you can. Learning how to do this is what the rest of this chapter is about.

For a neater look when you mail your application or résumé, use a 9″ × 12″ envelope—your papers will stay flat.

The Job Application

Job applications are forms that employers give to job seekers to fill out. Most job applications ask for personal information, such as name, address, phone number, and social security number. **Social security numbers** are assigned by the federal government for tax purposes. (To get a social security number, apply to the Department of Health and Human Services, Social Security Administration. You can find the nearest office by looking under the federal government listings in the front of your phone book.) Job applications may also ask about your health and citizenship. Most applications include sections on education and work experience as well.

At first, filling out a job application may seem like a simple task. After all, a job seeker just fills in the blanks. However, many job seekers become nervous when applying for jobs. They make mistakes, forget important information, and feel foolish. To make the job application process go smoothly, try using these tips:

1. *Ask for two applications.* If you're allowed to, take the applications home to fill out. Do a rough version on one copy. Mark it up as much as you wish. Save the second one for a clean final copy.

2. *Read over the application before you begin.* The application will tell you whether to write in pencil or pen. It will also tell you whether to print or type.

3. *Fill out the first copy of the application.* Make sure all the blanks are filled in except where you see the words "For Employer Only."

Date _____

Employment Application

Name	Phone No
Address	How long at this address
Social Security #	Are you a citizen of the U S
Position for which you are applying	Second Choice
Starting Salary Required	Starting Salary Desired

Explain any health condition or physical handicap which could affect your ability to perform the type of work for which you are applying

How much time have you lost from work or school in the past two years	Type of illness
Our work schedule is 8 00 a m to 5 00 p m Monday—Friday Are you able to conform to this work schedule?	What was the source of your referral to this company?

Names of friends & relatives with this company

In case of emergency, contact (name, address, phone #, relationship)

Education	College	Other
Name of School		
Address		
Dates Attended		
Grade Average		
Major		
Minor		

Are you studying now?

What?	Where?

For clerical personnel
Skills: Shorthand (_____ WPM)   Typing (_____ WPM)   Adding Machine (Touch Yes [ ] No [ ])
Others

Have you ever served in a branch of the U S armed forces, and if so, please list branch of service, your rank, and dates of service

To what professional, civic or social organizations do you belong (excluding those which indicate race, religion, or national origin)?

What are your principal hobbies?

Personal References: Name	Address	Business	Years Acquainted

On a job application, you may see these words: For employer only. *Do not fill out the information in that section.*

4. *Make sure all the information is correct.* Double check all spelling. If spelling isn't one of your best skills, give the application to a teacher or job counselor. Ask that person to look it over and make corrections.

5. *Copy the information from the first copy of the application onto the second.* If the application must

be typed, and you aren't a typist, give it to someone who is. Neatness counts!

6. **Proofread** *the final copy one more time.* If you need to make any final corrections, be sure to do so neatly. Use white correction fluid if you have it.

Careers Practice

Answer these questions on a separate sheet of paper.

1. How should you look when you go to apply for a job?

2. What are four pieces of personal information usually asked for on job applications?

3. Where can a job seeker apply for a social security number?

Writing a Résumé

A **résumé** is a written statement that includes a job seeker's work experience, accomplishments, education, and personal information. It is a statement of who you are, where you've been, and where you want to go. In many ways, it is your accomplishments and career plan in another form.

The résumé should be neatly typed on clean white paper. It should include only true information. If it doesn't, it can reduce your chances of getting a job to zero. Experts say that résumés should be no longer than two pages. One page is better. The shorter the résumé is, the more quickly an employer can tell if you're qualified.

Résumés can be organized in different ways. Most, however, include the following sections:

- *Personal information.* Résumés usually begin with the job seeker's name, address, and phone number.

You can pay someone else to write your résumé. However, this can sometimes cost more than $100.

- *Job objective.* This is the job you're applying for right now. For example: part-time salesperson.
- *Education.* Include where and when you went to school. If you graduated or received a certificate, mention it. Include the month and year that you graduated.
- *Work experience.* Besides the jobs for which you have been paid, this can include any unpaid or volunteer work. List the most recent experience first. Try to show your accomplishments in a measurable way. For example, instead of writing "served food," write "served food to 200 people during three-hour lunch shift."
- *Skills.* These are the things you know how to do well and that will help you do the job you want to get. Computer skills, communication skills, mechanical skills, and more can be listed here. Again, it is helpful to be specific. Don't just write, "computer skills." Say exactly what kind of computer and computer programs you know how to use. For example, "Can operate Macintosh computer; skilled in WordPlus word-processing software."
- *References.* Here you can list people who will speak for your character and work abilities. You can list their names, addresses, and phone numbers. You can also simply write, "Available upon request." Before giving people's names as references, be sure to ask their permission to do so. Tell them an employer may call to ask about you.

Now look at the résumé that Cathy used to apply for the part-time job in the clothing store. It's on the next page.

Catherine Johnson
777 Mitchell Street, Apartment A
Northway, Michigan 48167
(313) 555-4227

Objective   Part-time sales position in fashion clothing store

Education   Currently enrolled in Northway High School.

Due to graduate June 1997.

Work Experience   *6/96: Model*

Modeled clothing for community fundraising event.

2/96 to 5/96: Costume Design Assistant

Assisted in clothing design for school play; sewed costumes.

1994 to present: Babysitter

Work weekends and nights caring for children aged 6 months to 8 years.

Skills   Sewing, clothing coordination, basic math operations, excellent customer service skills.

References   Available upon request.

Cathy had no prior work experience other than babysitting. However, her unpaid work experience is important.

Learn More About It: Action Verbs

Whenever possible, use **action verbs** on your résumé or job application. Action verbs describe actions in a lively way. "Run," "write," "direct," and "plan" are some examples of action verbs. Action verbs give punch and color to your résumé. They also let you say a lot in a short space. Here are examples of how you can improve what you have to say by using action verbs to describe your accomplishments:

Without Action Verbs	With Action Verbs
Was a babysitter.	*Cared* for two children.
Have animals.	*Raised* prize dogs from puppies
Went to high school.	*Graduated* from high school.
Had a story in the school paper.	*Wrote* and *published* a story in the school paper.

Here are some other helpful action verbs for job seekers:

assembled	improved	prepared
built	interviewed	reported
coached	led	reviewed
cooked	listed	sent
delivered	managed	supervised
fed	operated	tested
filed	placed	updated
gathered	planned	wrote

The Cover Letter

A **cover letter** is a short letter that is sent with a résumé. It is an opportunity to emphasize why you are sending the résumé. It also gives the résumé a more personal touch.

When you write a cover letter, include your own name and address at the top of the paper. Then address the letter to the person in the company who has the power to hire you. Include the job title you are applying for, the skills or experience you have, and why you want to work for the company.

Cover letters should be short and to the point. A few paragraphs is all you need. Look at the cover letter that Cathy included with her résumé. It's on page 268.

Sending a cover letter with your résumé makes a much better impression than sending your résumé alone.

Careers Practice

Answer these questions on a separate sheet of paper.

1. What is a résumé?

2. Besides work for which you have been paid, what can "Work Experience" include?

3. How long should a cover letter be?

Catherine Johnson
777 Mitchell Street, Apartment A
Northway, Michigan 48167
(313) 555-4227

Fred Carlson
Manager, Women's Clothing Department
Narain's Department Store
1233 Main Street
Northway, Michigan 48167

September 15, 1996

Dear Mr. Carlson,

I am applying for the part-time sales position in your store. My résumé is enclosed.

I am currently a senior in high school. I plan to attend Northway Community College next year to learn more about clothing design and retail sales. Someday I hope to have a career as a fashion designer. Working part-time at Narain's would greatly help me move toward my long-term career goal.

I have excellent fashion sense and love both people and clothes. I believe I would make a good salesperson, and I hope you will give me an opportunity to work for you.

I look forward to hearing from you soon.

Sincerely,

Catherine Johnson

Catherine Johnson

Cover letters help make a résumé more personal.

Chapter Review

Chapter Summary

- There are several ways to increase your chances of successfully applying for a job. One way is to apply in person. Dress neatly in clean clothing. Project a positive attitude. Get all applications and résumés in on time. Make sure they are complete, correct, and neat.

- A *job application* is a form that employers ask job seekers to fill out. Applications ask for personal information, job experience, and skills.

- A *résumé* is a written statement of work experience, skills, and personal information. It usually includes the job objective, information about education, and references. Good résumés are neatly typed. They list accomplishments in a measurable way and use action verbs.

- A *cover letter* is a short letter that is sent with a résumé or application. It is a way to make a résumé more personal. It is also an opportunity for the job seeker to point out qualifications that will help him or her get the job.

Chapter Quiz

Answer these questions on a separate sheet of paper.

A. Thinking About Careers

1. Why is it important to make applications and résumés complete, correct, and neat?

2. What is a social security number?

3. If you don't have a social security number, where can you apply for one?

4. Why is it a good idea to fill out job applications at home?

5. What are four things found on a résumé?

6. What color paper should a résumé be typed on?

7. How long should most résumés be?

8. What should be included in the education section of a résumé?

9. What could you list under references?

10. What is a cover letter?

B. Putting What You Learned to Work

Suppose you're applying for a part-time job. It could be at a fast food restaurant, in an office, or anywhere you choose. Put together a first draft of a résumé that you would use to apply. Include all the major sections described on page 263–264.

C. Work Out

Now write a cover letter for your résumé. Make up the name and address of the person and business you're writing to. Use the cover letter on page 268 as a model.

Chapter 21

Interviewing for Jobs

Job seekers should dress carefully and neatly for job interviews.

Chapter Learning Objectives

- Explain the purpose of a job interview.
- List three ways to prepare for a job interview.
- Tell what to do after a job interview.
- Describe how to make the most of not getting a job.

Words to Know

annual report   a book or pamphlet published yearly that describes an organization and its accomplishments

mission   purpose

public relations department   a department that is responsible for giving out information about an organization

---

Rachel had just interviewed for her first job as a library assistant. Her friend Shelly came over to ask her about it.

"So how did it go?" Shelly asked. "Did you get the job?"

Rachel shrugged. "I won't know for about a week."

"Well, how do you *think* it went?"

Rachel thought for a moment. "I went there prepared," she said. "I answered all the questions the best I could. The strange thing was—"

"What?" Shelly asked.

"Well, I'm not really sure I *want* the job. I thought I'd be working more with people. It turns out that 80 percent of the job is putting books back on the shelves."

"What's the other 20 percent?"

"Taking books *off* the shelves," Rachel laughed. "From the job description I read, I thought I'd work at the information desk for a few hours each week. Still, I do love books, and I think the library would be a fun place to work. It would be good experience, too."

Shelly laughed. "It sounds like the employer isn't the only one who has to make a decision."

What Job Interviews Are For

Shelly and Rachel have just learned an important lesson about job interviews. The purpose of the interview is to help both the employer *and* the job seeker come to a decision. The employer is deciding if the applicant is the best person for the job. Will he or she fit in? Can the applicant do the job? Will the person be on time and do good work? Employers will usually interview at least three people and then choose from among them.

Job seekers use the interview process to convince employers to hire them. They also use the interview to decide whether the job is right for them. Rachel discovered that the library assistant's job wasn't exactly what she'd had in mind. She, too, must decide if the match is right.

Some people find job interviews tough. Others know that interviewing is a skill that can be learned. Preparing for the interview is an important part of learning that skill.

How to Prepare to Answer Questions

An interview is a question-and-answer session. The first step in preparing for an interview is guessing what the questions will be. The next step is practicing the answers.

Employers can ask dozens of questions in dozens of ways. However, most job seekers should be prepared to answer at least three questions:

1. Why do you want to work here?

2. Are you qualified?

3. Why should I hire you instead of someone else?

By asking these questions—in one way or another—employers are trying to find workers who will fit in. They are looking for people who can

Ask a friend who has interviewed for a job what it was like. What did the employer ask? How did your friend answer?

contribute. They want employees who will "get behind" what their organizations do. They want team members who will help their organizations succeed.

How do you show an employer that you are that person? Begin by researching the organization. Go to the human resources department or the **public relations department** of the company. Ask for **annual reports**, newsletters, or articles about the

To prepare for a job interview, practice asking and answering questions.

organization. Your library might also have clippings about the company. Try to talk to a current employee or to someone who has done business with the organization.

Once you find sources of information, take notes. Find out what the **mission** (purpose) and goals of the organization are. Decide what you like most about the organization. Memorize facts about its size and history. Find out what you can about the organization and what it might be like to work there. Armed with this information, you can better prepare yourself to answer questions.

Employers sometimes ask if you have any weaknesses. Answer honestly, but also tell how you make up for them.

Next, carefully review your accomplishments. Be prepared to talk about your strengths. The interview is a time to showcase your talents and abilities. The employer may ask about your personality and work style. Show your best side, but be honest. If you like working with *things* more than people, say so. Remember, you want a job that will match who you are.

You will also have to make a case for why you're the best person for the job. Be prepared to talk about what you will do. Outline what your goals would be. For example, "If you hire me, I will work to provide your customers with the best service in town." Or, "If you hire me, I will become your best repair person within six months. I'll be productive and do good work." Again, be honest in what you want to do. Be positive and enthusiastic about your future.

How to Prepare Your Own Questions

The interview is also your time to ask questions. Some job seekers memorize the questions they want to ask before the interview. Others write the questions down and bring them to the interview. In either case, you are showing the employer that you're prepared.

Some questions you might want to ask:

1. What kind of projects or duties will I have?

2. What would you like the person in this job to achieve?

3. What opportunities might the future hold if I do this job well?

4. When will you be deciding whom to hire?

5. When do you want the person you hire to start?

Quite often, the employer will answer these questions during the interview before you ask them. Be prepared, however, just in case. It is a good idea to limit your list to ten or fewer questions.

What other questions might you ask during an interview?

How to Practice for the Interview

You've done your research. You've made up your list of questions. Now it's time to practice for the interview.

Some people feel silly practicing for job interviews. Don't. Practice is very important. Athletes train for games. Actors rehearse for plays. Politicians try out their speeches. Job seekers must practice just as these people do if they want to do their best. A successful job seeker is one who has practiced.

There are several ways to do this. You can read your questions and answers into a tape recorder and then play them back. You can interview yourself in the mirror. You can also ask a friend to play the part of the employer. When you practice, follow this list of dos and don'ts:

If you have access to a video camera, tape yourself practicing the interview with a friend. It will help you make sure your expressions and gestures look friendly and natural.

- *Do* pronounce your words in a strong, clear voice. *Don't* mumble or put your hand over your mouth.

- *Do* keep your answers short and to the point. They should last no longer than two minutes.

- *Do* make eye contact. *Don't* stare.

- *Do* smile occasionally. *Don't* grin or frown.
- *Do* nod your head up and down thoughtfully. *Don't* look away or down.
- *Do* use your hands in an open, friendly way. *Don't* cross your arms, wring your hands, or tap your fingers.
- *Do* sit up straight. *Don't* slouch.
- *Do* keep your legs together and your feet flat on the floor. *Don't* shake your feet.

If you find yourself shaking, stumbling over answers, or forgetting things, don't worry! Now is the time to improve. Practice as much as you need to. Each time you do, you'll get a little bit better.

Careers Practice

Answer these questions on a separate sheet of paper.

1. What is the purpose of the job interview?

2. What three questions are employers likely to ask in one form or another?

3. How can a job seeker get information about an organization?

How to Present Yourself

The day of your interview comes. You've practiced and practiced. Now it is time to put the finishing touches on your interview.

Take a quick look at yourself right now. Are you dressed for a job interview?

To make a good impression, dress neatly. Your clothes should be clean and pressed. Don't wear anything flashy. Shower and comb your hair neatly. Brush your teeth and wear deodorant. Stay away from strong perfumes and aftershaves.

Be ten minutes early for the interview. Employers want workers who will be on time. If you're late, you aren't likely to get a second chance. When the employer greets you, shake his or her hand warmly. Say how nice it is to be there!

Before and during the interview, practice breathing deeply. This will help you relax. Once in a while, check to see how you're sitting. If one of your legs is shaking wildly, or you're slumped in your chair, stop it. Sit up tall. Try to be calm and relaxed. Remember to smile.

As you ask and answer questions, let your positive attitude shine through. Remember that this is one of the key things employers look for. Keep your answers short—at the most, two minutes. At the end of the interview, shake the employer's hand again. Say thank you and ask when you might hear about the job.

Writing a Thank-You Letter

Sometimes, an employer will hire a person at the time of the interview. This, however, is rare. Employers usually like to think over their decisions. They weigh the pros and cons of the candidates they've interviewed. Sometimes it takes them weeks to make a decision.

As a job seeker, you want to go on making a good impression even after the interview. One way to do this is to write a thank-you letter. This shows that you have good manners. It also reminds the interviewer that you are enthusiastic about the job.

Address the thank-you letter to the person who interviewed you. Be sure to spell the person's name correctly. Restate your interest in the job and briefly say why you're the right person for the job. Thank the employer for his or her time. Write and mail the thank-you note immediately after the interview. Do not let more than a day go by. The employer will be impressed with how quickly you followed up.

```
                    Rachel Lee
                  120 Park Street
              Harris, New York 90021

                  (313) 555-1111


Linda Tilly, Librarian
Harris Public Library
21 Green Street
Harris, New York 90021

                      June 4, 1998

Dear Ms. Tilly,

Thank you for the time you spent
interviewing me yesterday. I am very
interested in the position of library
assistant. As I told you, I believe
the library offers an important
service to the community. I believe my
love of books and my attention to
detail qualify me for the position. I
would be proud to be on your staff.

I look forward to hearing from you
soon.

                    Sincerely,

                    Rachel Lee

                    Rachel Lee
```

Here is a typical thank-you letter sent after an interview.

Making the Most of Not Getting a Job

The interview is over. You've sent the thank-you letter. Now you must be prepared to get the job— or to *not* get it.

Being prepared to get the job is easy. You thank the employer. You find out when and where to start working. Then you hang up the phone and have a party to celebrate.

What do you do if you *don't* get the job? The most important thing is to get information from the employer about why this happened. Call the employer when you're not feeling sad or angry. Politely ask what you could have done differently to get the job. Again, thank the employer and ask him or her to keep you in mind for future openings. Use any information you get from the employer to prepare for your next interview.

Rachel Lee, for example, didn't get the library assistant's job. The librarian sent Rachel a letter saying someone else had been selected. Rachel waited two days so that the disappointment couldn't be heard in her voice. Then she called the librarian. This is how the conversation went:

Rachel: Ms. Tilly, this is Rachel Lee. I just received your letter saying I wasn't chosen for the job. I wondered if you could answer a few questions that would help me in my future job search.

Ms. Tilly: Sure, Rachel.

Rachel: How could I have been better qualified?

Ms. Tilly: Well, the person I chose had done volunteer work in her school library. Also, I really had the sense that you would be happier working more with people.

Rachel: You're probably right. Could I improve my interview skills in any way?

Ms. Tilly: You interviewed quite well. I did notice that you were disappointed that you wouldn't be working with people much.

Rachel: I see. Well, thanks again, Ms. Tilly. Please keep me in mind if a position comes up that you think is a good match for me.

Ms. Tilly: I will, Rachel. Good luck.

Some employers don't return phone calls after notifying job seekers that they haven't been chosen. If this happens to you, accept it. There's nothing you can do about it.

From this talk, Rachel learned that, like herself, Ms. Tilly wasn't sure that Rachel would enjoy the job. Rachel also learned that volunteer experience could have improved her chances of getting the job. She also learned that she had let her disappointment show during the interview. This is something she can work on. Rachel can use the information she has received to help her get another job.

Careers Practice

Answer these questions on a separate sheet of paper.

1. What are three ways to practice for a job interview?

2. How should you dress for a job interview?

3. What should you do immediately after a job interview?

Learn More About It: Visualizing Success

It is the day before a big swim meet. A champion swimmer sits quietly by the pool. He sees himself growing taller, his arms and legs stretching. Now he imagines himself diving into the pool. His stroke is perfect. He passes the other swimmers with ease. He wins the match.

The swimmer is doing what many successful people do. He is visualizing success. Visualizing helps to build confidence. It is another form of practice.

To visualize your success in a job interview, close your eyes. Take a deep breath. See your relaxed smile. Hear your strong, clear voice. Listen to your thoughtful, well-prepared answers. Now visualize the handshake and the nod of the employer. Hear the employer say, "You've got the job."

Chapter Summary

- The purpose of a job interview is to help both the employer *and* the job seeker make a decision. The employer decides who is the best person for the job. The job seeker uses the interview to convince the employer that he or she is the best person. The job seeker also uses the interview to decide whether the job is right for him or her.

- Employers want the answers to three basic questions: Why do you want to work here? Are you qualified to do the job? Why should I hire you instead of someone else? To answer these questions, job seekers should research the companies they are thinking about working for. They should also prepare themselves to talk about their strengths and future goals.

- Before interviews, job seekers should practice asking and answering questions. They should pay attention to what they say, how they say it, and how they look.

- During interviews, job seekers should appear relaxed, alert, and friendly. Looking neat and being on time are quite important.

- After interviews, job seekers should follow up immediately with thank-you letters.

- To make the most of not getting a job, the job seeker should contact the employer with whom he or she has interviewed. The job seeker should ask what he or she could improve upon for future interviews.

Chapter Quiz

Answer these questions on a separate sheet of paper.

A. Thinking About Careers

1. Does getting an interview mean that a person has been hired?

2. What is an employer deciding during a job interview?

3. What is a job seeker deciding during a job interview?

4. What are three questions usually asked in job interviews?

5. When researching a company, what should you try to find out?

6. What is one way to practice asking and answering questions?

7. Why is it important to be on time for an interview?

8. How should you sit during an interview?

9. When should you send a thank-you letter?

10. Suppose you're turned down for a job. The employer says you did not have enough experience. How can you make the most of this information?

B. Putting What You Learned to Work

Imagine that you are interviewing for a job that fits your career plan. The employer asks, "Why should I hire you?" Write down what you would say. Keep your answer short—no more than two paragraphs.

C. Work Out

Imagine that you are the employer. Write down a list of things that you would like to see in an employee. Consider dress, habits, and personality. Do you meet your own expectations? Explain in a short paragraph.

Unit Six Review

Answer these questions on a separate sheet of paper.

1. How long can you expect a job search to last?

2. Give three examples of people with whom you can network.

3. Where can you find want ads?

4. What two types of employment agencies offer services free of charge?

5. Why is it helpful to fill out job applications at home?

6. What is a résumé?

7. What are references?

8. What is one way to prepare for an interview?

9. Terri is going to a job interview for a receptionist's position at a computer company. Should she wear a miniskirt and high heels, or should she wear a business suit? Why?

10. What should you do if you do not get a job for which you have interviewed?

Success on the Job

Chapter 22
Learning a New Job

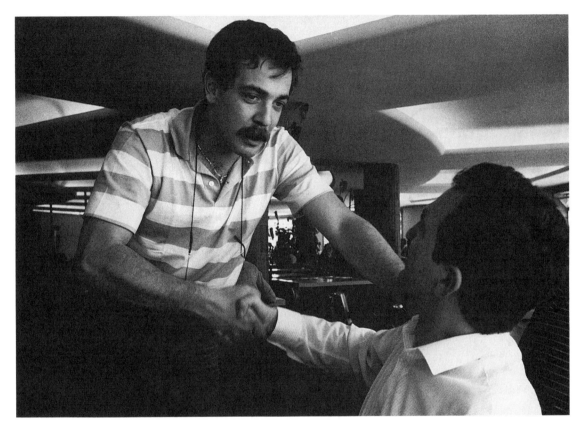

Beginning a new job can be fun and exciting.

Chapter Learning Objectives

- Tell how having a good attitude can help a worker who's learning a new job.
- List three ways to keep motivated on the job.
- List ways to learn new job skills and remember information.
- Describe helpful job resources available at most companies.

Words to Know

cosmetology   the study of make-up, hair styling, and other beauty techniques

customer service representative   a worker who provides information and solves problems for customers

employee handbook   a book or booklet that gives workers important information about the company that employs them

memorandum   a short written notice (*memo* for short)

motivated   inspired to do something

peer mentor   a person who has the same job responsibilities as another, but who is more experienced and can offer advice about the job

policy   a general rule or philosophy about how things should be done

procedure   a step-by-step outline of how a task is to be performed

recreation aid   a worker who helps organize sports, crafts, games, and other enjoyable activities

retain   to keep or hold onto

role model   a person who is admired, respected, and imitated by others

---

It was an evening in late June. Harlan was on the back porch rocking back and forth in his grandmother's chair. He was trying not to think about the next day. Harlan was going to start a summer job as a **recreation aid**. He would be helping to run activities for young children at the city park.

Harlan's grandmother came out to sit with him. "Is something bothering you?" she asked.

"No," Harlan lied.

His grandmother nodded. "It's a big day tomorrow, isn't it?" she said, almost to herself. "New job and all."

Harlan knew he couldn't hide anything from his grandmother.

"You know," he said, "when I got this job I felt great. I was on top of the world. Now I'm scared. What if the kids don't like me? What if I make a fool of myself? What if I fail?"

"Harlan," his grandmother replied, "there's an old saying that goes, 'You are what you eat.' Well, I believe you are what you *think,* too. If you think you'll fail, you probably will. Do you remember why you wanted this job? You love working with kids, and this experience will help you become a youth counselor later on. And don't forget the money you'll earn. Keep those thoughts in mind and you'll be fine."

Harlan watched his grandmother as she rose and walked back into the house. Suddenly, he felt foolish. He stood up, stretched, and headed inside.

"Are you going to bed early?" his grandmother asked.

"Yes. I've got to be rested if I want to do well."

"You always were smart," she said.

Harlan didn't say anything. He knew who was the smart one in the family. He kissed his grandmother goodnight.

Attitude and Motivation

How do you feel when you're in a new situation?

Beginning a new job, at any age, can be stressful. Many people worry about how well they will do in new situations. They wonder what their co-workers will be like. They wonder about their job duties. They're afraid of being laughed at or even fired.

These feelings are natural. However, there are some things you can do to make beginning a new job less stressful. In Chapter 17, you read how important it is to have a positive attitude. A positive attitude can help make a new job an adventure.

Harlan started his job looking forward to the things he would learn. Then, at times when he doubted himself, he thought of his strengths. When he made mistakes, he thought of them as problems to be solved. He asked his co-workers for help. In time, Harlan became a favorite among the children he worked with. His co-workers liked him, too. By the end of the summer, he received a raise. The city offered him a part-time job during the school year. He had moved a few steps closer to his career goal.

Having a positive attitude can get you off to a good start. Here are some practical steps you can take to keep yourself **motivated** to do well.

- *Be clear about exactly what you are supposed to do.*

New workers often feel frustrated if they are unsure of their duties. If you are confused about what is expected of you, talk to your supervisor. Ask questions until you know exactly what to do. Don't wait to make mistakes.

- *Do things well.*

Jim is a sculptor. He sometimes spends more than a year making a statue. When he is finished, he takes great pride in what he has done. The work, as well as the knowledge that he did something well, gives him energy. He is motivated to continue.

When you start a new job, make an effort to always do the best you can. Like Jim, you may find that the work itself gives you pleasure.

- *Look for recognition from others about a job well done.*

Some companies are very good about recognizing and rewarding their employees. They give "Employee of the Month" awards, raises, and praise to those who do well. However, bosses are not always good at rewarding their employees. Sometimes you'll have to ask, "How am I doing?" It also helps to get feedback from other employees or from customers. For example, Harlan was motivated when the children thanked him for what he did for them. Their recognition made him feel good. They gave him a reason to show up for work each day.

- *Think of your work as valuable to the company and to yourself.*

Sometimes you may feel that your job is not "important" enough. When this happens, remember that a company's most important resource is its workers. It cannot run without them. It also helps to remember that your job is just one step on your career plan. If it is helping you get where you want to go, it is valuable.

- *Look for ways to grow.*

What kinds of things motivate you to do a good job?

At some point, you may become comfortable in your job. But if you become *too* comfortable, the job may become boring. You may not be motivated to do well. Always look for new ways to be creative. Volunteer for new duties. Offer suggestions on how the work can be done better. Doing these things will help keep you doing your best and loving your work.

Careers Practice

Answer these questions on a separate sheet of paper.

1. What kind of thoughts can cause stress to someone who is starting a new job?

2. What is one thing a person can do to lessen this stress?

3. What can recognition for a job well done do for a worker?

Training on the Job

Most companies provide their workers with the training they'll need to do their jobs. The kind of training a worker gets depends greatly on that worker's past experience and also on the particular job he or she will be doing. Jane, for example, became a

customer service representative for a bank after she graduated from high school. Bank customers could call 24 hours a day to get information about their accounts and the bank's services. Jane's job was to answer their questions and solve their problems.

Before beginning her job, Jane spent three weeks in a classroom. There she learned how to use the bank's computers. She learned about banking services. She also learned how to treat customers and how to solve their problems. At the end of the training, she took a test. After she had passed it, she began her regular job.

Tony's training was not as structured as Jane's. Tony was a warehouse worker for an office supply company. His job was to read orders, package supplies, and ship them out. When new supplies came in, Tony would record them, unpack them, and store them in the warehouse. Tony learned his job from another warehouse worker. He watched and helped the other worker for a day, asked questions, and then began working on his own. When he forgot what to do, he went back to his co-worker for advice. Once in a while, a supervisor came by to check Tony's work.

While a company may provide training, it is still up to you to do the learning. A number of things can help you **retain** information. For example, new employees are often told to read **employee handbooks** or training manuals. These resources contain **policies** and **procedures** that workers should know about. Such books may contain a great deal of information— much more than you could ever memorize.

If you are asked to read such a book, take notes as you read. Mark sections that you think you'll need to look at again. If you don't understand something, ask your trainer or boss about it. Remember, being clear about what you're supposed to do will help you stay motivated.

Have you ever been trained on the job? If so, describe your experience to a classmate who has never worked.

Role models and peer mentors can also help you learn on the job. A **role model** is a person you admire who is respected at work. He or she does things the right way. If you find a role model, watch how this person behaves. Study his or her work habits. Listen to how the person talks to co-workers and customers. By imitating your role model, you can learn important skills.

A peer mentor is a little different from a role model. A **peer mentor** is an experienced person who has the same responsibilities that you have. Like a role model, the peer mentor is respected for his or her work. However, the peer mentor is also someone you can readily go to for advice. He or she can "show you the ropes" of doing your job.

Finally, there's no better way to learn a job than to do it. At the very least, be on time and put in a full day's work. Be willing to put in extra time if you can. Study training manuals and the employee handbook on your own time at home. If you work for a good company, your extra effort will be noticed. Also, you'll feel good knowing that you're doing the best work you can.

More Helpful Resources on the Job

Most companies provide workers with other resources that can help the workers do their jobs. For example, large companies have human resources (personnel) departments. Human resources departments help hire new workers. They also assist new workers with learning about policies, programs, and benefits. In later chapters, you'll learn more about human resources departments and the roles they play.

Another helpful resource is the **memorandum** (*memo* for short). Memos are written notices to workers. Sometimes a memo will communicate

Could a role model or peer mentor help you in school?

Company newsletters are another helpful resource. They include news about employees, changes in the company, and upcoming company events.

Job aids can help you remember important information.

something simple, like the date and time of a company picnic. Sometimes it will contain more serious information, such as an important policy change. It is your responsibility to read all memos and know how they affect your work. Most bosses will not accept the excuse, "But I didn't read the memo." They want workers who are alert and aware.

Most companies also provide resources that help their workers keep track of their duties. For example, companies where people work different shifts post new work schedules every week. Work schedules list who is working and at what time. If your company uses work schedules, it is up to you to read them and remember your assignments. Sometimes it helps to take a copy of the schedule home.

Likewise, companies will often provide job aids to help workers do their jobs better. A job aid could be

Look for job aids in the classrooms or halls of your school. What are they?

a sign that says, "Wear your safety equipment at all times." Another job aid could be a sample of a form already filled out. The worker uses this form as a model. Still another job aid could be a wall calendar that shows the schedule for a project. Other job aids might list postal rates, the prices of products, and so on. The purpose of a job aid is to help a worker find information quickly and to do a better job. Noticing these jobs aids—and using them—makes a worker more independent and efficient.

	M	T	W	Th	F
Abrams, J.	8–1	8–1	12–5	8–1	12–5
	AM PM	AM PM	PM PM	AM PM	PM PM
Kelly, M.	12–5	12–5	8–1	4–8	4–8
	PM PM	PM PM	AM PM	PM PM	PM PM
Scott, C.	6–10	6–10	6–10	12–5	8–1
	PM PM	PM PM	PM PM	PM PM	AM PM

This work schedule tells us that J. Abrams is working from 12 P.M. to 5 P.M. on Wednesday.

Careers Practice

Answer these questions on a separate sheet of paper.

1. What is an employee handbook?

2. What is a role model?

3. When a memo goes out to workers, what should they do with it?

Learn More About It:
Using a Personal Calendar

Cindy had just started a part-time job as a hair stylist. At the same time, she was taking classes to get her **cosmetology** license. Cindy soon found that she had too many things to remember. She was missing classes, showing up late for work, and not doing a good job.

Cindy began using a personal calendar to keep track of where she had to be each day and what she had to do. The calendar looked a bit like a notebook. Each page listed a different week of the year. At the beginning of the week, Cindy wrote down her class and work schedules. She also wrote in her homework assignments, the phone numbers of her customers, and social events. She even penciled in the time she allowed to clean her bathroom! She looked at the calendar each morning to remind her of the day's events. Whenever necessary, she updated it to include any changes.

Cindy is still quite busy. However, she no longer misses classes or gets to work late. Her customers are happy, and so is she. She feels more in control and does a better job both at school and at work.

Chapter Review

Chapter Summary

- Beginning a new job can be a stressful experience. To lessen this stress, workers should start new jobs with positive attitudes. They should look forward to learning and having new experiences. They should view their jobs as important steps toward their long-term career goals.

- Workers can and should take responsibility for staying motivated. Some ways to do this are to understand your duties, do things well, look for recognition, value your work, and look for ways to grow.

- Most companies provide new workers with some training. The kind of training differs with an employee's past experience and with the work he or she will be doing.

- Asking questions and taking notes can help you learn a new job. Imitating a role model or asking advice of a peer mentor can also be helpful.

- New workers can learn more about their jobs through their companies' human resources departments. They can also learn through memos, newsletters, and job aids. Using job aids can help workers become more independent and efficient.

Chapter Quiz

Answer these questions on a separate sheet of paper.

A. Thinking About Careers

1. How can having a positive attitude affect stress?

2. What are three things a worker can do to stay motivated on the job?

3. Do all workers get the same kind of training on the job? Explain.

4. What kind of information do employee handbooks contain?

5. If an employee handbook is too large to memorize, what can you do?

6. What kind of person makes a good role model?

7. How can a peer mentor help a new worker?

8. What kinds of questions can human resources departments answer for new workers?

9. Why should workers always read memos?

10. Give an example of a job aid.

B. Putting What You Learned to Work

The same things that motivate people at work can motivate students in school. Write a list of three things you can do to stay motivated in school. Look back at the first few pages of the chapter for ideas.

C. Work Out

Make a calendar for this week. List your classes, social events, and job schedule if you're working. Also include homework assignments and other things you need to accomplish. See if it helps you stay on track.

Chapter 23

The Work Environment

Being on time every day is an important job skill.

Chapter Learning Objectives

- Describe how income taxes are collected.
- Explain fringe benefits.
- List safety measures that companies must follow.
- Tell how union membership works.

Words to Know

agency shop   a business in which employees are not required to join a union but must pay union dues

contract   a verbal or written agreement made between two or more people or groups of people

fringe benefits   any benefits given to workers other than wages, such as vacation pay, sick leave, health insurance, pensions, and so forth

Internal Revenue Service (IRS) the bureau of the U.S. Treasury Department charged with enforcing the tax laws passed by Congress

net income   money earned minus the amount withheld

Occupational Safety and Health Administration (OSHA)   the federal agency that is charged with inspecting businesses and enforcing safety laws

right-to-work laws   state laws that give people the right to work without having to belong to unions

tax return   a worker's report to the government of how much the worker has earned, paid in taxes, and either owes in taxes or is due in a tax refund

union shop   a business in which all non-management employees must be union members

W-2 form   a yearly wage and tax statement sent by a business to an employee

W-4 form   a statement that determines the amount of taxes withheld from an employee's paycheck

withhold   to keep or hold back

It was a Friday evening. Charlene had just walked in the door with her first paycheck in her hand. She didn't look happy.

"What is it?" her father asked. "I thought you'd be excited about making a little money."

Charlene sat down. "Well, I am, Dad. It's just that I'm not making as much as I thought I was."

"What do you mean?" her father asked.

Charlene handed him her paycheck stub. "Just look what they've done."

Her father studied the amounts listed. "The company has taken out your fair share of taxes. If you didn't pay them now, you'd have to pay them later. You'd better get used to it, darling. It's part of working."

Charlene took back the paycheck stub. "I suppose," she said. "I just wish that I'd been expecting it. I thought I'd have more income to save and to spend. I may have to put off those night classes for another year."

Being Prepared for the World of Work

Charlene went to work without knowing how businesses handle their employees' taxes. She received an unpleasant surprise that may cause her to rework her career plans.

At one time or another, all workers experience surprises on their jobs. A swimming pool cleaner in Los Angeles is asked to clean out a pool filled with gelatin used in a TV commercial. A police officer tries to coax an environmentalist out of a tree that is scheduled to be cut down. A delivery driver presents flowers to a sick gorilla in a city zoo. These are surprises that no one can quite prepare for.

There are, however, some common things in the work environment that shouldn't surprise you. One of them is taxes. Others are benefits, safety practices, and unions. Knowing what these things are and how they work can help you prepare for the reality of the workplace.

Taxes

When you go to work for a company, you enter into a contract. A **contract** is an agreement. You agree to perform certain duties. In return, the company agrees to pay you a certain amount of money.

Workers and employers have another type of contract with their federal, state, and local governments. By law, businesses and workers must pay taxes to the government. In return, the government provides certain goods and services. For example, the government provides police and fire protection, medical care for the poor, and public schooling.

To keep this contract with the government, businesses and their employees use a basic, four-step process. Here is how it usually works:

Step 1. When a company hires an employee, the employee fills out a **W-4 form**. The purpose of this form is to find out how much in taxes the company should **withhold** from the employee's paycheck.

Form **W-4** Department of the Treasury Internal Revenue Service	**Employee's Withholding Allowance Certificate** ▶ **For Privacy Act and Paperwork Reduction Act Notice, see reverse.**	OMB No. 1545-0010 19**93**

1	Type or print your first name and middle initial	Last name	**2** Your social security number

Home address (number and street or rural route)	**3** ☐ Single ☐ Married ☐ Married, but withhold at higher Single rate. **Note:** *If married, but legally separated, or spouse is a nonresident alien, check the Single box.*
City or town, state, and ZIP code	**4** If your last name differs from that on your social security card, check here and call 1-800-772-1213 for more information · · · · ▶ ☐

5	Total number of allowances you are claiming (from line G above or from the worksheets on page 2 if they apply) .	**5**	
6	Additional amount, if any, you want withheld from each paycheck	**6**	$
7	I claim exemption from withholding for 1993 and I certify that I meet **ALL** of the following conditions for exemption:		

- Last year I had a right to a refund of **ALL** Federal income tax withheld because I had **NO** tax liability; **AND**
- This year I expect a refund of **ALL** Federal income tax withheld because I expect to have **NO** tax liability; **AND**
- This year if my income exceeds $600 and includes nonwage income, another person cannot claim me as a dependent.

If you meet all of the above conditions, enter "EXEMPT" here · · · · · · · · · · · ▶ | **7** |

Under penalties of perjury, I certify that I am entitled to the number of withholding allowances claimed on this certificate or entitled to claim exempt status.

Employee's signature ▶   Date ▶   , 19

8 Employer's name and address (Employer: Complete 8 and 10 only if sending to the IRS)	**9** Office code (optional)	**10** Employer identification number

The human resources department or your supervisor can help you fill out your W-4 form.

Whether you are single, married, a student, or have children can affect the number of *allowances* you get. The more allowances you have, the less tax is withheld. The W-4 is used by the company, and a copy is on record with the government.

Step 2. The company pays the worker but withholds the taxes. The company might also take out money for a retirement plan, health insurance, and so on. The company supplies the worker with a paycheck and a paycheck stub. The paycheck stub gives the details of earnings and taxes. **Net income** is what employees sometimes call "take-home pay." It is the money earned minus the amount withheld.

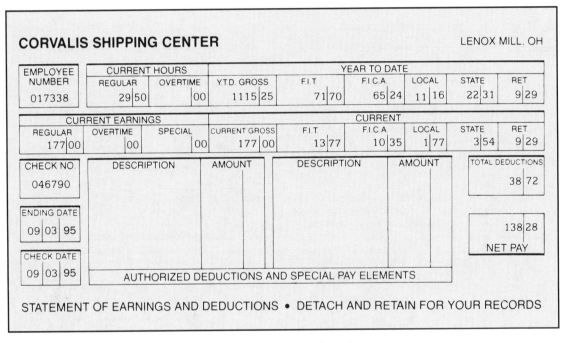

Read your paycheck stub carefully to learn what is taken out.

Paycheck Vocabulary

Here are some abbreviations and terms that you may find on paycheck stubs and tax forms.

F.I.C.A.	social security tax (the letters stand for Federal Insurance Contribution Act)
F.I.T.	federal income tax
gross pay	the total amount of money you earned in the pay period
local	local taxes, such as those paid to a city or county
net pay	How much you've earned after all your withholdings or deductions have been taken out. This is your take-home pay. It is the actual amount of money your check is worth.
overtime	hours or pay *over* your usual rate
pay period	the time period for which you are being paid
regular	hours or pay *at* your usual rate
ret	retirement fund
social security tax	tax put into a fund that is used to provide income to people who are retired or unable to work and to their families
state	state taxes
wages, tips, and other compensation	total income
Y.T.D.	year-to-date

1 Control number		OMB No. 1545-0008		

2 Employer's name, address, and ZIP code	3 Employer's identification number	4 Employer's state I.D. number
Freeman's Medical Supplies 1523 86th Street Dixon, CA 95620	5 Statutory employee ☐ Deceased ☐ Pension plan ☐ Legal rep. ☐	942 emp. ☐ Subtotal ☐ Deferred compensation ☐ Void ☐
	6 Allocated tips	7 Advance EIC payment

8 Employee's social security number 999-00-3534	9 Federal income tax withheld $336.70	10 Wages, tips, other compensation $2,900.00	11 Social security tax withheld $207.38
12 Employee's name, address, and ZIP code Maria Ramirez 3123 Rosedale Road Dixon, CA 95620	13 Social security wages $2,900.00	14 Social security tips
	16	16a Fringe benefits incl. in Box 10
	17 State income tax $78.06	18 State wages, tips, etc.	19 Name of state
	20 Local income tax	21 Local wages, tips, etc.	22 Name of locality

Form **W-2 Wage and Tax Statement** **1993**
This information is being furnished to the Internal Revenue Service

Copy B To be filed with employee's FEDERAL tax return   Dept. of the Treasury—IRS

Box 9 of this W-2 form shows the amount of federal taxes withheld. Box 10 shows total income for the year.

The United States has a "graduated tax system." The more you earn, the higher the percentage of taxes you must pay.

Step 3. At the end of the year, the company sends the worker a statement of wages. It is called a **W-2 form**. The form includes the total amount of income the worker earned that year and the taxes that were withheld by the company.

Step 4. Each year, by April 15, all workers must file state and federal income **tax returns** for the previous year. That means that if you worked in 1996, you would have to file tax returns by April 15, 1997. The simplest tax return asks workers to list their total income and the total amount paid in taxes. If the company withheld too much in taxes, the worker gets a tax refund. If the company withheld too little, the worker has to mail a check to the government for the amount owed.

The tax laws in the United States can change from year to year. It pays to try to understand them. Some large companies offer tax advice to their employees. Other workers can go to an accountant or tax adviser for advice. The government bureau that enforces tax laws, called the **Internal Revenue Service (IRS)**, offers free information on taxes. You can contact your local office of the IRS for a list of resources.

Fringe Benefits on the Job

Earlier you read that some employers offer their employees fringe benefits. **Fringe benefits** are any benefits given to workers other than wages. They include such things as vacation pay, sick leave, health insurance, pensions, and so forth.

It makes sense for a worker to understand what benefits are offered and how to use them. Philip, for example, is a repair technician for an electric company. He learned that his company had a tuition reimbursement (payback) plan. If Philip took job-related classes, his company would refund the money it cost him to take the classes. Philip was thus able to get more education. Not only did he get his tuition money back, he got promoted because of the new job skills he learned.

Other common fringe benefits that may be offered by a company include:

Health insurance. With most health insurance plans, the company and the employee each pay a certain amount every payday. When the employee goes to a doctor, all or part of the bills are paid by the health insurance plan. Sometimes an employee's family can be included on the health plan, too. This usually costs more.

In the 1990s, health insurance is an important concern for most workers. Health care has become so expensive that many companies have stopped offering it. Other companies offer limited health insurance that doesn't cover all types of treatment. Some companies offer several health plans. The plans vary in costs and in the services they provide.

Dental insurance. This works the same way health insurance does, but it is for teeth and gum care.

Sick leave. Some companies allow employees a certain number of paid sick days per year. Sometimes the employee can "save" these sick days and carry them over from one year to the next.

Vacation leave. In the United States, many companies offer two weeks of paid vacation each year. Usually, you cannot use this vacation time until after you've worked for a full year.

Pension or retirement plan. Some companies withhold a certain amount from each paycheck for the employee's retirement. The company invests this money. When the employee retires or leaves the company, he or she gets the money back in a lump sum or in monthly payments. As with all fringe benefits, pension plans can vary greatly from company to company.

Careers Practice

Answer these questions on a separate sheet of paper.

1. What is a W-4 form?

2. What is a W-2 form?

3. What is a tuition reimbursement plan?

Safety on the Job

Lydia is an environmental technician. She works for a company that tests soil for toxic substances. Lydia wears gloves, safety glasses, and protective clothing when she works. One day she went into the field without her glasses. She phoned her supervisor. "I've got to come back," she said. "I forgot to bring my glasses."

"No. Stay and do the test," her supervisor replied. "We promised the client we would have it done today."

Lydia's supervisor gave her bad advice. In 1970, the federal government passed a law called the Occupational Safety and Health Act. It requires all employers to provide a safe and healthy workplace. This means providing safe equipment, protective clothing when needed, and education about safety practices.

OSHA, the **Occupational Safety and Health Administration**, is supposed to inspect companies and enforce safety laws. However, OSHA is not big enough to do the job. Since 1970, as many as 200,000 workers were killed on the job in the United States. Two million more died from diseases caused by the conditions where they worked.

What does that mean to you and your career? As a worker, you have the right to a safe work environment. You also have to take some responsibility for enforcing that right. If you are a new worker, ask to enroll in any safety classes offered by the company. If no class is offered, insist that you get briefed in safety practices. If you are around chemicals, poisons, cleaners, or machinery, ask how they should be handled safely. If a company provides you with seatbelts, hardhats, or other safety equipment, use them. Even people with "safe" jobs should learn about fire exits and basic safety rules such as not walking on wet floors.

Finally, you should watch your co-workers. See that they follow any safety rules and practices the company has. If they do not, remind them that your safety could be threatened by a mistake that they might make. If they continue to ignore safety practices, inform a supervisor. Doing so could save a life.

The Bureau of Labor Statistics says that 25 percent of all on-the-job injuries occur during the first six months of employment.

Unions

When you become an employee, you may be asked to join a union. You already learned about trade unions in Chapter 10. However, labor unions also exist for office workers, teachers, and many other kinds of workers. Unions are groups of workers organized to get and maintain decent wages and working conditions. Becoming a member of a union means that you will have to pay union dues. These union dues go toward supporting the union and the work it does.

Whether or not you choose to join a union depends on several things. Some businesses are called **union shops**. If you work in a union shop, you must join the union within a certain period of time. This is usually 60 or 90 days after you start working. In an **agency shop**, employees are not required to join a union. They still have to pay union dues, though. In states that have **right-to-work laws**, workers do not have to belong to unions or pay union dues.

If you are free to join or not join a union, you must consider what unions do. The fringe benefits you read about earlier are due in large part to the efforts of unions over the years. However, some people believe that unions have outlived their usefulness. Others say that unions drive up the costs of goods and services by demanding higher pay.

Right now, about 16 percent of all workers belong to unions. If you are asked to join a union, learn as much as you can about it. Then decide if it is right for you.

Careers Practice

Answer these questions on a separate sheet of paper.

1. What agency helps enforce safety laws in the workplace?

2. Since 1970, about how many workers have been killed on the job?

3. If you work in an agency shop, do you have to join the union? Explain.

Chapter Review

Chapter Summary

- Among the things workers should know about are taxes, benefits, safety practices, and unions.

- All businesses and workers must pay taxes in return for government services. Businesses withhold taxes from employees' paychecks on a regular basis. At the end of the year, the company sends the employee a W-2 form. It shows how much the employee has been paid and how much has been withheld in taxes. The employee then files a tax return.

- Companies may or may not offer fringe benefits. It is up to the employee to learn what benefits are offered and how to use them. Some common fringe benefits are health insurance, dental insurance, sick leave, paid vacations, and pension or retirement plans.

- All workers have the right to a safe work environment. Employers should provide safe equipment, protective clothing when needed, and education about safety practices. Workers must sometimes take the responsibility to see that these things are supplied and used.

- Labor unions exist for many types of workers. Several things could influence a worker's decision about whether to become a union member. These include state laws and the worker's thoughts and feelings about unions.

Chapter Quiz

Answer the following questions on a separate sheet of paper.

A. Thinking About Careers

1. What are three types of services that citizens get in exchange for paying taxes?

2. What is net income?

3. By what date must workers file their yearly tax returns?

4. What is the IRS?

5. How does health insurance work?

6. When are employees usually able to take two weeks of paid vacation?

7. What is OSHA?

8. What should you do if you get a job working around chemicals, poisons, cleaners, or machinery?

9. Are unions for trade workers only? Explain.

10. What are right-to-work laws?

B. Putting What You Learned to Work

How would you most like to see your tax dollars used? Write a short paragraph explaining your answer.

C. Work Out

If you could have only two of the fringe benefits discussed in this chapter, which two would you choose? Why? Write a short paragraph explaining your answer.

Chapter 24

Working with People

Successful people know how to get along with their co-workers.

Chapter Learning Objectives

- Explain what is meant by the term *work ethics*.
- Explain the benefits of working as a team.
- Describe laws that entitle workers to fair treatment.
- List steps used to solve problems at work.

Words to Know

authority   the power or right to give orders and make others obey

discrimination   unfair treatment because of one's race, color, religion, or sex

entitle   to allow or give right to

ethics   a system of rules or principles of behavior

minority   a member of a group that makes up less than 50 percent of the population

national origin   the country where a person was born

sexual harassment   any unwelcome sexual advances or conduct

James felt lucky. He'd been hired as a helper on a road crew. His friend Terry had recommended him for the job.

One day after work, Terry gave James a ride home. When James got in the car, he noticed a power drill on the backseat. It was one they used on the job.

"Hey, isn't that power drill from work?" he asked Terry.

"It sure is," Terry replied. "Let's just say I'm borrowing it."

"Did you ask the boss? Mr. Scott said all the tools were to be locked up at night."

"Relax," Terry said. "I'll come in early tomorrow and return it.

He'll never know it's gone."

The next day at lunch, Mr. Scott called the crew together at lunch time.

"We're missing some tools," he said. "A power drill, a jack, and some shovels are gone. Does anybody know where they are?"

James looked at Terry. Terry winked.

If you were James, what would you do?

That night, James couldn't sleep. He knew what had happened. He just didn't know what to do.

People and Problems on the Job

A big part of being successful on any job is getting along with co-workers. Co-workers include everyone from the boss on down. The workers in most companies are like any other group of people. Sometimes they work as a team. They get along well and have fun. But sometimes their work suffers until they find a way to handle their problems.

This chapter is about how to prevent problems such as the one facing James. It is also about handling the problems that can't be prevented.

Work Ethics

James must decide what to do about Terry. He knows Terry has done something wrong. James must decide what his own responsibility is. He must think about his work ethics. Work **ethics** are rules that are used to help workers decide how to behave in their jobs.

Deciding what is right and wrong can be a very personal matter. However, there are basic rules that apply to most work situations. Following these rules can help prevent problems in the workplace. For example, you read in the last chapter that workers have an agreement with their employers. The workers agree to perform certain duties to the best of their abilities. In exchange, the employers agree to pay them for their labors. A simple work ethic is to live up to this agreement. Provide an honest day's work for an honest day's pay. Doing your share of the work will help you earn your co-workers' respect.

Another good work ethic is to respect your boss's **authority.** A supervisor's duty is to watch an employee's work. If an employee is not working up to standards, then the supervisor will try to get him or her to improve. If your boss is being reasonable, it is up to you to follow his or her direction. Complaining, grumbling, or not following directions will only create ill feelings.

Workers should also respect the property that's owned by the companies they work for. Some employees take home office supplies such as pens, pencils, and paper. They use company phones for personal long-distance calls. Or, like Terry, they help themselves to tools or other equipment. These people do not always think they're stealing. However, they have no right to borrow, take, or use property without permission.

Finally, it is important to treat your co-workers with respect. Being polite, offering your help, and being a good listener are important on the job. Most co-workers will respect you if you respect them. Together, you can work as a team.

What other rules would you add to your work ethics? Why?

Teamwork

What does it mean to work as a team? How can it add to your success in the workplace? Here's an example:

Sylvia worked as a teacher's aid at a preschool. Her job was to do art projects with the children every day. Sylvia thought up some great projects. However, she couldn't get the children to listen to her. During her art class, the kids ran wild.

The head teacher saw that Sylvia was having problems. "I've assigned a volunteer to help you," she told Sylvia. "This person is very experienced in handling children. See what you can learn from him."

Sylvia resented the volunteer at first. His name was Mr. Sanders. He was 74 years old. "What can that old man teach me?" she thought to herself.

Mr. Sanders soon showed her. His calm and loving manner attracted the children. He was firm with them when they misbehaved. Because they liked him, they gathered around him during art class. Soon they began listening to Sylvia.

By looking for and valuing each other's strengths, people can be more productive members of a team.

Finally, Sylvia realized how valuable Mr. Sanders was. "I'm glad you're here," she said. "I'd be a failure without you."

"Oh, no," laughed Mr. Sanders. "Without you, *I'd* be a failure. I could never keep these kids busy the way you do. All I do is get them to calm down. The fact is, we're a great team."

That day, Sylvia saw the benefits of working as a team. She realized that each of us has certain strengths. By pooling our strengths, we can be productive and efficient.

Being a good team member will become even more important in the coming years. As you read in earlier chapters, the U.S. work force is changing. Women are playing a greater role than ever before. **Minorities** are taking new leadership roles in business and government. With the help of technology, disabled Americans are able to work in many different jobs. Today's work force as a whole is growing older.

As a young worker coming into this work force, you must look for and value your co-workers' differences. You must recognize the unique strengths that each person brings to the workplace. In return, your co-workers will value what you have to offer. Together, you can work as a team to provide fresh ideas and ways to do things better. Everyone will benefit!

Careers Practice

Answer these questions on a separate sheet of paper.

1. What are work ethics?

2. Give an example of a rule that all workers should follow.

3. How can working as a team help people be more productive?

Your Right to Fair Treatment

Manuel is a worker with good ethics. He puts in his fair share of work every day. Whenever the boss asks him to, he works overtime. He likes his co-workers and is well respected by them. His boss is always telling him that he is the most skilled worker on the team.

When a supervisor's position opens up, Manuel applies for the job. He has all the qualifications. Then Manuel learns that someone with less experience than he has is going to get the job.

Manuel's supervisor pulls him aside. "You know, it's nothing personal," she says. "It's just that you're a minority here. Most of the workers have backgrounds that are different from yours. I'm afraid there will just be trouble if you become a supervisor. I'm sure you understand."

Manuel has just become a victim of job **discrimination**. Because of his ethnic background, Manuel was not promoted.

The law in the United States requires employees to treat all workers fairly. One of the most important laws to affect workers is the Civil Rights Act of 1964. It states that no employer can use race, color, religion, sex, or **national origin** as a reason to hire, not hire, fire, or promote employees. The Civil Rights Act of 1964 **entitles** workers to fair treatment. Under the law, it would have been legal to not promote Manuel if he was a bad worker or couldn't do the job. But it was illegal to deny him the promotion because he was Latino.

Another important law recently passed is the Civil Rights Act of 1991. It entitles workers who believe they are victims of racial discrimination or **sexual harassment** to sue their employers in court. If the victim wins, the employer could have to pay the victim money.

What exactly is harassment? Suppose Joan's supervisor asks her for a date. Joan politely turns him down, saying she would prefer not to. The next day, Joan's boss asks her out again. She nicely explains that she isn't interested. A week later, Joan's boss tells her that the company is doing poorly. He might have to let some of the office workers go. He tells Joan that if she goes out with him, he will see that she keeps her job.

This kind of unwelcome pressure is one example of sexual harassment. Making unwanted sexual comments or touching a person in an unprofessional way are also examples of sexual harassment. Sexual harassment has become a big issue in the 1990s. Recent surveys say that roughly 40 percent of women report having been sexually harassed in the workplace. Occasionally, male workers complain of being sexually harassed as well.

Some high schools have rules to protect students against sexual harassment. Do you think such rules are needed in schools?

What to Do About Problems at Work

Most of the time, problems at work can be solved among co-workers. James, for example, talked to Terry about the missing tools. He told Terry to return them. If he did not, James said he would have to tell the boss what he knew. Terry was angry, but he returned the tools.

Unfortunately, many problems are more complicated and not so easily solved. A teenager is fired for having a tattoo. A female police officer quits the force because her male co-workers believe a woman can't do the job, and they tell her so. A qualified 50-year-old worker is let go because he is "too old." An African-American man who is highly qualified is passed over again and again for promotions.

In such cases, what should workers do? Quite often, workers simply quit jobs in which they are being treated unfairly. They do not believe it is worth the time, money, and trouble it might take to fight their employers. This is their right.

Other workers believe they should fight for fair treatment. In such cases, workers should be prepared to state the facts. For example, they could keep written records of what is said or done to them. The written record should include dates and times as well. Whenever possible, another person should be aware of the trouble the person is experiencing. This person can later testify in court if necessary.

In large companies, workers can make complaints to their human resources departments or to their unions. Quite often, a company or union will have a set of policies and procedures on how to handle such complaints.

Other workers take their complaints directly to the EEOC. *EEOC* stands for the Equal Employment Opportunity Commission. This federal government agency investigates written charges of discrimination against employers. If the EEOC finds the charges to be true, it will try to reach an agreement between the employee and employer. If no settlement is reached, the EEOC may bring charges against the employer in federal district court. However, the EEOC is not always quick to act. It receives about 60,000 employment discrimination cases each year. In 1990, only 640 cases went to court.

You read earlier that current civil rights laws allow workers another option. They can take employers to court themselves. However, undertaking any kind of court action is a big task. It takes time, energy, and money. There is no guarantee that the worker will win the case. Before taking such a step, a worker should talk to a lawyer who specializes in employment law.

You may never have to face such decisions. You may give and receive fair treatment throughout your career. However, should problems arise, you will have to make a choice about what to do. Your decision will depend on your own ethics and the situation you face. Thinking about such things now can better prepare you for the future.

Careers Practice

Answer these questions on a separate sheet of paper.

1. Can an employer fire a qualified worker because of his or her race?

2. What law prohibits this kind of practice?

3. A man puts his arm around his co-worker's shoulder in what he sees as a friendly way. She has asked him several times not to touch her at all. What could this be an example of?

Learn More About It:
The Americans with Disabilities Act

Frank is a bank teller. He does his job just as his co-workers do. He counts cash, deposits money, and sells traveler's checks. He is judged by the same standards as his co-workers. He works his fair share for a day's pay. The only thing different about Frank is his teller window. It is lower and wider than the other windows. It allows Frank to work in his wheelchair.

Frank and thousands of other disabled people now have a special law protecting them from discrimination. The Americans with Disabilities Act (ADA) was passed July 31, 1990. It affects companies with 25 or more employees. Under the law, employers cannot discriminate against people with disabilities. Employers must also offer "reasonable accommodations" for disabled workers to do their jobs. Frank's special window is one example of how an employer changed the workplace for a disabled worker. Wheelchair ramps, enlarged computer screens, and amplified phone lines can help other disabled workers perform their jobs.

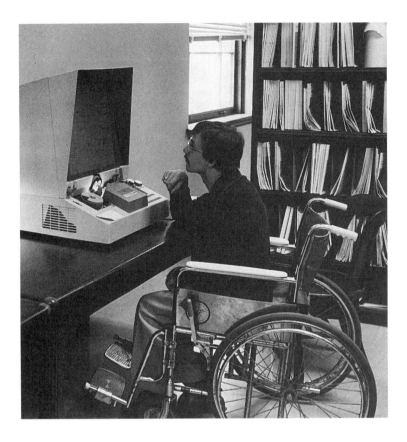

The ADA requires employers with 25 or more employees to equip their workplaces for disabled workers.

Chapter Review

Chapter Summary

- Successful people know how to get along with their co-workers. They learn how to prevent problems and to handle problems that can't be prevented.

- Workers can prevent and handle problems by having good work ethics. Some work ethics are a matter of personal choice. However, all workers can benefit from doing the following: provide an honest day's work for an honest day's pay; respect the boss's authority; respect company property; treat co-workers with respect.

- Employees can benefit by working as a team. They should look for and value each other's strengths and differences. They should pool their strengths to be more productive and efficient.

- Employers are required to treat workers fairly. Civil rights laws and the ADA prohibit employment discrimination on the basis of race, color, religion, sex, national origin, or disabilities.

- Problems on the job must be handled in a case-by-case manner. An employee could speak directly to a person who is causing him or her a problem. He or she could also speak to the human resources department, a union, or the EEOC. Employees also have the right to take employers to court.

Chapter Quiz

Answer these questions on a separate sheet of paper.

A. Thinking About Careers

1. What are work ethics?

2. How should workers respond to their supervisor's directions?

3. How should workers treat the property at work?

4. What is one benefit of working as a team?

5. What law tries to prevent employers from discriminating against workers on the basis of race, sex, or religion?

6. What recent law allows workers to take employers to court for sexual harassment?

7. What does the ADA make illegal for employers to do?

8. What is the EEOC?

9. If a worker believes she is being treated unfairly, what kind of record should she keep?

10. If a worker is being treated unfairly, is it acceptable for him to quit? Explain.

B. Putting What You Learned to Work

Write your own work ethics guidelines. List at least five rules that will help you decide how to behave on the job.

C. Work Out

Think of three people who are very different from you, especially in how they work. List at least one strength of each person that you admire. Then write a short paragraph about how these strengths could be valuable to a work team.

Unit Seven Review

Answer these questions on a separate sheet of paper.

1. What is one thing a new employee can do to lessen stress on the job?

2. Do all new employees attend training classes? Explain.

3. What book or booklet usually contains important company policies and procedures?

4. How can a role model help a person learn a job?

5. What federal agency enforces tax laws?

6. Give three examples of benefits found on the job.

7. What federal agency helps ensure worker safety?

8. If a state has right-to-work laws, can you be forced to join a union?

9. What are work ethics?

10. What does the EEOC investigate?

Lifelong Learning

Chapter 25

Using the Job Review as a Learning Tool

The job review is an important tool for your career.

Chapter Learning Objectives

- Explain the purpose of job reviews.
- Tell what a performance standard is.
- Describe three things that can affect performance.
- List three opportunities to explore during job reviews.

Words to Know

attainable able to be gained or achieved

career path a map or outline of how a worker could move or advance in a company

evaluation a judgment of performance, such as a job review

exceed to go beyond what is expected

job review an evaluation of an employee by an employer

lateral transfer a sideways move within a company to a different department or to a different position at the same level of salary and responsibility

probation a trial period

quarterly every four months

standards set guidelines

Jane Murray woke up one morning with butterflies in her stomach. While getting dressed for work, she decided to clean her apartment before leaving. She washed the dishes, dusted the bookcase, and swept the floor. When Jane's roommate Alice came down for breakfast, she found Jane rearranging the cereal boxes.

"What's wrong?" Alice asked.

Jane shrugged. "What do you mean what's wrong? I'm just cleaning up."

Alice grabbed a box of cereal from Jane's hand. "Whenever you're nervous, you start cleaning like a madwoman. Now what's wrong?"

Jane moved on to wiping the spice shelf. "My boss at the travel agency said she wants to talk to me today. She said, 'Be prepared for our talk tomorrow. I'll see you first thing in the morning.' I've only been there three months. Could she want to fire me already? I'm not quite as fast as my co-workers, I know that. But I thought I was doing OK."

"Three months?" Alice asked. "You're getting your three-month job review. That's normal. Nearly everybody gets one. Relax."

Alice put down her cleaning rag. "Job review? What's that for?"

Alice grabbed her coat. "You'll find out. I'm late, gotta go."

Alice opened the door and then stopped. She turned to Jane. "One last thing, Jane," she said.

"What's that?"

"Do my room next."

The cleaning rag hit the door just as Alice closed it.

How Job Reviews Work

Job reviews are sometimes called "performance reviews" or "performance appraisals."

The job review is a learning tool that can help you be successful in your career. It can help you know how you are doing on the job. It can help you improve your performance.

A **job review** is an employee **evaluation**. The employer judges areas such as attendance, attitude, and how well job-related tasks have been performed. In most companies, a new employee has a job review after three months. Until that time, the employee is on **probation**. The probation period is a trial time for the employer and the employee to determine whether the job and the worker fit. After the first job review, this evaluation may be done every four months (**quarterly**) or once a year.

As a rule, the employer will use set **standards** by which to judge the employee. For example, in Jane's company, it was considered normal for an employee to be absent or late an average of once every other month. Since Jane had a perfect attendance record, she got a high rating in this area. She **exceeded** the standard. In most job areas, Jane met the standards. She did just what the job required. However, Jane was slow in getting customers their airline tickets. In that area, she received a "needs improvement" rating.

Quite often, the employer will use a job review form to rate the employee. Here's the form that Jane's employer used:

Escape Travel

Employee: Jane Murray　　Supervisor: Liza Leano

Position: Travel agent　　Review: 3-month review

	Needs Improvement	Meets Standards	Exceeds Standards
1. attendance			X
2. attitude			X
3. relationships with customers			X
4. ticketing procedures:			
on time	X		
accuracy		X	
flexibility		X	
5. research abilities		X	
6. relationship with peers		X	
7. relationship with supervisor		X	
8. meets training requirements		X	

This is one example of a job review form.

Using the Job Review Process

Some people dread job reviews. Like Jane, they think that all they'll hear is bad news. However, a worker who takes an active role in the job review may find it to be a useful tool. How do you make the job review process work for you?

How do you think an employer could measure an employee's attitude?

Begin by knowing exactly what the performance standards are for your job. A good performance standard is measurable. You'll be able to know whether or not you've met it. Jane's boss told her she should have all the customers' tickets ready the same day or the day after their travel plans were set. Jane sometimes took two or three days to get the tickets ready. So she didn't meet the standard. She knew she was slow even before the job review.

A good performance standard is also **attainable.** It is *possible* for you to meet it. Jane saw that all the experienced travel agents were able to issue tickets on time. With practice, she knew she could do the same.

Before you begin a job, ask your supervisor what the performance standards are. Know exactly what is expected of you. Ask if you can see a sample of the company's job review form. If there is something unclear on the form, ask about it. Let your supervisor know you want to do well.

Once you know the standards, you can work toward meeting them. Keep your own records if that helps. Every once in a while, ask your supervisor how you're doing. Ask what you're doing well and what you could improve. Don't wait until the job review.

A day or so before your job review, prepare. Write down a list of the things you want to talk about. Your performance does not have to be the only subject. If you've done something really well on the job, tell your boss about it. If there are things you'd like to do better, bring them up. If you've made mistakes, be prepared to talk about why they happened. Let your boss know you're evaluating yourself on the job.

Careers Practice

Answer these questions on a separate sheet of paper.

1. What are three ways in which a job review can help you?

2. What are two qualities of a good performance standard?

3. Why is it a good idea to know the performance standards before you begin a job?

Solving Problems in the Job Review

What happens during the job review? As a rule, the supervisor will probably go over the items on the job review form point by point. He or she will explain your ratings and why you earned them.

It is easy to hear about the things we do well. If you're exceeding or meeting standards, be proud! However, remember that a job review is also a place to deal with problems. Listen to what your supervisor has to say. If there are areas where you fall short, think about why. There are three main things that keep people from meeting standards:

1. *Lack of skills or knowledge.* Suppose Jane had never been shown the fastest way to get tickets for her customers. All her co-workers used a shortcut that she didn't know about. In this case, it would be easy to improve her performance through training. If you're not meeting standards on a job, sometimes it helps to show your boss just what you are doing. He or she may be able to train or coach you to perform better.

2. *Something wrong in the work environment.* Suppose Jane had the oldest computer in the company. It was slower than the others. As a result, it took her much longer to order airline tickets. Perhaps this is

the reason she was not meeting the job standard. In this case, Jane's boss could either change the performance standard or get her a new computer. There are many things in the work environment that can hurt performance. Noise, co-workers who don't do their work, difficult customers, and poor equipment are just some of them. During your job review, discuss any such problems with your supervisor. Don't use them as excuses. Simply say that they are possible reasons why you're not working well. Then, along with your supervisor, try to find ways to improve the environment.

3. *Lack of motivation.* Suppose Jane had the knowledge and the skills to do the job. Her equipment worked fine. What was stopping her from doing well? Jane could have lacked the motivation to do the job. Many of the things that motivate people were discussed in Chapter 21. For example, people need to be recognized for their work. They need to feel their work is of value. If you lack motivation but have a good relationship with your boss, you might want to discuss your feelings in the job review. Good supervisors will often be able to offer suggestions.

Can you think of other common reasons why a person would lack motivation?

Exploring New Opportunities in the Job Review

Job reviews can also be a time to explore new opportunities within the company.

New opportunities come in many forms. Peter, a police officer, has been a street cop for 20 years. Yet he's always looking for new opportunities on the job. Over the years, he has served on a gang task force, done fundraising, and trained other officers. He has let his supervisor know that these new opportunities keep him excited about his work. When new opportunities come up, his boss goes to Peter first.

If you find yourself in a job you like but you want new challenges, let your supervisor know. Like Peter, you may be able to make valuable contributions to your company.

During the performance review, you can also ask your supervisor about career paths. **Career paths** are usually found in large companies. They are like career ladders. They outline or map how a person could advance or change jobs in a company to earn more or do something more interesting.

The career path for travel agents in Jane's company is shown on page 338. Inexperienced travel agents come in at the entry level. They handle family vacations and small trips. Agents must work at this level for at least two years before they can be promoted.

If they do get promoted, they can either become business travel agents or sales agents. Business travel agents arrange travel for large businesses. Sales agents try to get new accounts for the company. Both positions earn about the same income.

Notice in the figure that a person can go from being a business travel agent to being a sales agent. The reverse is also true. This is called a **lateral transfer.** A worker can move sideways to a different department or to a different position at the same level of salary and responsibility.

You know what a lateral transfer is. What do you suppose a lateral pass in football is?

Finally, the business or sales agent could become a team manager. The team manager supervises a group of travel agents or sales agents. It is the highest level a person can reach in that company.

Supervisors can usually help employees along a career path. They can direct employees to further training and experience that will help them get promoted. Use the job review to let your ambitions be known. Most people will appreciate your desire to get ahead and to learn new things.

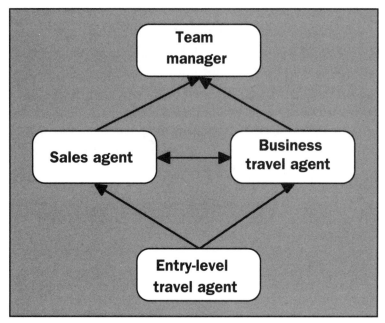

A career path at Escape Travel

Careers Practice

Answer these questions on a separate sheet of paper.

1. If a worker lacks the knowledge to do a job well, what can his or her supervisor do to fix the problem?

2. Karen takes orders on the phone. Her supervisor tells her that customers have complained that Karen yells at them. Karen apologizes. She also explains that she works beside some loud machinery. Sometimes she has to shout to be heard. How can Karen's problem be fixed?

3. What is a career path?

Learn More About It:
One Entrepreneur's Job Review

Paul O'Leary is an entrepreneur. He has his own landscaping business. He works with his customers to design their yards. He helps them figure out what plants they want, what their walkways or fences should look like, and so on. Then he puts the design on paper. When the design is approved, Paul calls in his work crew. He supervises the planting, building, and other work they do.

After a year in business, Paul felt something was missing. It was hard for him to know just what he was doing right. He sometimes wished he had a supervisor to evaluate him.

Then Paul got an idea. He decided to have his customers evaluate him. After all, they were the people who judged his performance every day.

Paul thought about the standards he wanted to meet. Then he put them on paper. At the end of each job, he asked his customer to fill in an evaluation form. Here are some of the questions it asked:

1. Did I always meet my deadlines?

2. Was I always polite and courteous?

3. Did you find I had good knowledge of plants?

4. Overall, what did you like about my work?

5. In which areas do you think I could improve?

Paul could now get a better idea of what he was doing well. He could also target things he needed to do better. Paul had found a creative way to handle job reviews.

Chapter Review

Chapter Summary

- Job reviews are evaluations. They can help us improve our performance, solve problems, and explore new opportunities.

- Most companies have standards by which they judge employee performance. A good performance standard is measurable and attainable.

- Employees should know what the performance standards are before they begin their jobs. Then they can work toward meeting them. Employees should take an active role in the job review by preparing questions and information beforehand.

- When an employee does not meet standards, the supervisor and employee should figure out why. It could be due to lack of skills or knowledge, something wrong in the work environment, or lack of motivation. Once the reason is pinpointed, the supervisor and employee should work to correct it.

- Job reviews are a good time to explore new opportunities. The employee can ask about extra projects, career paths, and transfers.

Chapter Quiz

Answer these questions on a separate sheet of paper.

A. Thinking About Careers

1. What is a job review?

2. How often do job reviews occur?

3. What do employers use to judge an employee's performance?

4. What two qualities should all performance standards have?

5. What is one way in which workers can take an active role in the job review?

6. What are three main things that keep workers from meeting standards?

7. If a person lacks the skills to do a job, how can that be corrected?

8. If a person is not performing to standards because a machine keeps breaking down, how can that be corrected?

9. What is a career path?

10. What is a lateral transfer?

B. Putting What You Learned to Work

Think of a time when your performance was not up to standard in school or work. What do you think caused it? Think back to the three main reasons for performance problems discussed in this chapter. What could have been done to improve your situation?

C. Work Out

Write three performance standards for a job. Make sure the performance standards are both measurable and attainable.

Chapter 26

Changing with the Times

Changes in our lives may cause changes in what we need from our careers.

Chapter Learning Objectives

- Show how personal choices and unplanned events can affect career plans.
- Tell how changing human needs can affect career plans.
- List five ways to continue lifelong learning.
- Review the career planning process.

Words to Know

alimony   any regular payment of money due to a separated or divorced person from his or her spouse

audit   in education, to listen to or attend a class without being officially enrolled

genealogy   the study of a family history or family tree

hierarchy   a ranking of things according to importance

self-actualization   a state of development that is reached when a person achieves his or her goals

theory   an explanation of or ideas about a subject

When Michael was in high school, he dreamed of being a rock and roll star. He took music in school and played in a band on weekends. When he graduated, he packed his bags and headed west.

"I'm going to Los Angeles," he told his friends. "That's where it's all happening."

Michael found the City of Angels an exciting place. He got a small apartment and shared it with a friend. Soon, however, he found that he couldn't make enough money to support himself by just playing music. So he got a job as a security guard. For four nights a week, he guarded a warehouse. On two nights, he played in small clubs. During the day, he wrote music and networked, trying to make connections in the music business. Three years later, Michael was still playing his music in small clubs. He was still working as a security guard, too. The only difference was that Michael had fallen in love. He wanted to get married. He thought he might even like to have kids.

Michael took a walk to the beach one day. Something was bothering him. He still loved music, but becoming a star didn't seem so important to him anymore. He wanted a steady income, a home, and a family. He knew that, feeling as he did, his career plans would have to change.

Being Prepared for Change

Back in Unit One of this book, you read how important it is to be flexible. Technology, world events, and the changing population all influence the job market. For example, hundreds of workers are employed at a typewriter factory. Then the factory owners realize that computers have made typewriters outdated. They decide to close the factory for good. Another company moves its factory to a country where labor costs are lower. A hospital builds a new wing for older patients. A whole new staff of health professionals is needed to run it. Outside factors have forced the workers in each of these situations to revise their career plans.

There are other factors that can equally affect our career plans. They are personal choices, unplanned events, and our changing human needs. This chapter is about those other factors. It is also about how to prepare for the changes.

What is the latest piece of new technology you have seen or heard about? How could it affect the job market?

Personal Choices and Unplanned Events

Long ago, when Michael was in high school, he made a career plan. His long-term goal was to be a rock and roll star. He did his research and found that the odds of becoming a star were slim. He decided to work toward his dream anyway.

Now Michael is changing. He's finding that there are things in his life that he had not counted on. Until this time, he had never seen himself as a husband or father.

As you grow older, you'll make some personal choices that could change your life. Unplanned events that you have no control over can also change your life. In either case, you must be prepared to revise your career plan. Here are a few of the things you may encounter:

Marriage. Getting married may be the farthest thing from your mind right now. It could also be that you're planning to get married right out of high school. In either case, marriage can cause you to revise your career plan. Michael, for example, didn't want to work every night of the week. His soon-to-be wife worked days, and he wanted to spend time with her in the evenings. He adjusted his career plan in such a way that would help his marriage succeed. As it turned out, Michael went back to school to get a teaching degree. He became a music teacher at a local high school.

Married couples find many different ways to have careers and still be happy together. Some find it better to work different shifts. Then when they're together, they enjoy each other more. Others feel it's important to spend more time together at home. They like to share dinner each night and talk over the day's events. When the time comes for you to marry, you will have the task of seeing that your career plan is something your partner can live with. If not, you may have to make some adjustments.

Children. As you read in Chapter 13, having children can be seen as a career choice. Children need the attention and love of their parents. Juggling the demands of home and work can be difficult. The cost of child care can also affect the amount of money you must earn. Having children and working is not impossible. It just means making choices wisely.

Divorce. Divorce can be a personal choice or an unplanned event. Sometimes, two people agree that it's best to split up. Sometimes, one person wants the divorce and the other doesn't. In either case, divorce can have a big effect on career plans, especially for women.

Have you seen how people's careers and lifestyles change as they grow older? How?

In 1991, only 15 percent of divorced or separated women were awarded **alimony** payments. This means that most divorced women were expected to work and support themselves. In some cases, a woman with children may get some child-support money from her husband. However, some fathers fail to make the payments on time—if at all. In either case, divorce can become a financial strain for both parties. It could change what they need from their careers.

Sickness or disability. No one plans on getting sick or having a disabling accident. However, as you read in Chapter 23, thousands of people are injured or become sick each year as a result of their jobs. Thousands more become ill or disabled because of events that are not job-related. When this happens, people must revise their career plans.

Our Changing Human Needs

Your career plan will also need to be revised as you grow and mature. As people become older, their values and human needs change. Many psychologists have studied how people and their careers change with age. One of them, Dr. Abraham Maslow, had this **theory**:

Maslow said that people have five basic human needs. We attempt to satisfy these needs in both personal and professional ways. Maslow ranked these five needs in a **hierarchy**. He said we start by satisfying our need for survival. This need is at the bottom of the hierarchy. Then we work through the higher levels of need. When we reach the top, we have attained our goals. At any time, unplanned events or personal choices may cause us to slip down or climb up the hierarchy. We might also work through the hierarchy several times in our lives. Some of us may never reach the top.

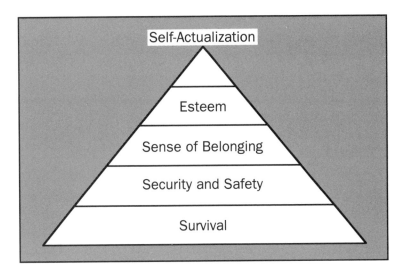

This is Maslow's hierarchy of needs in the form of a triangle.

Maslow believed that our first need in life is simply to survive. We are most concerned with having food, shelter, clothing, and health. When this need is present, we will probably take any job that gives us the income we need to live.

Once that need is satisfied, we look for safety and security. During this stage, we could look for a steady job with a steady income.

With a sense of safety and security well in hand, we develop a need to belong. We want good and lasting relationships with people. During this time, we may start a family. Professionally, we may seek to improve our relationships with our co-workers. We may also choose to do volunteer work in the community to satisfy this need.

We then move on to satisfy our need for esteem. We want respect from others, and we want to respect ourselves. We are more self-assured about who we are and what we want. At this time in our lives, we may feel brave enough to start our own business. Or we may try for a big promotion.

Once we feel this respect, we are able to work toward self-actualization. **Self-actualization** is the

Learn More About It: Climbing Maslow's Ladder

Kai was very proud when he graduated from trade school. He had a degree in computer repair. But to Kai's surprise, he couldn't find a job right away in his field. Kai took a job selling furniture in a department store. It paid the bills. It helped him survive.

Finally Kai got a job in a computer hardware company. He worked hard each week. He enjoyed the regular paycheck. He was safe and secure.

As time went on, Kai felt he wanted to be part of something bigger. He got involved with a group in his community that helped troubled kids. Kai loved this work. It gave him a sense of belonging. Around this time, Kai got married and started a family.

After several years, Kai felt the need for something more. He decided to start his own small business. He sold and repaired computers. He enjoyed the respect he got from his customers and employees. And he was proud of himself. He felt good about his life and who he was.

Kai is retired now. He is considered a leader in his community. People come to him for advice. When his grandchildren ask him if he has any regrets, he shakes his head.

"My goals were modest, but I achieved them," he says. "I will die a happy man."

point where we attain our goals. We are fulfilled, happy human beings. At this point, many people decide to make a major career change. They may find themselves at the bottom of the triangle again or somewhere in between.

Maslow's hierarchy is only one view of how our needs and values change. The most important thing is to be aware of how your human needs are changing as you grow older or have different life experiences. This will enable you to revise your career plans as needed.

Careers Practice

Answer these questions on a separate sheet of paper.

1. Give an example of a personal choice that could affect your career.

2. Give an example of an unplanned event that could affect your career.

3. Who was Dr. Abraham Maslow?

Lifelong Learning

The world changes. We change. What can we do to be prepared?

One of the most important things we can do is to engage in lifelong learning. Lifelong learning means many things. It is being aware of what is going on inside yourself. It is being aware of the world around you and how it is changing. Sharing new skills or sharpening old ones is also part of lifelong learning. Any time you try something new, you are learning.

Lifelong learning does not necessarily take place in a classroom. It can occur in many ways. Here are five things you can do throughout your life:

1. Read newspapers and magazines. Listen to and watch the news on radio and TV. Learn what is

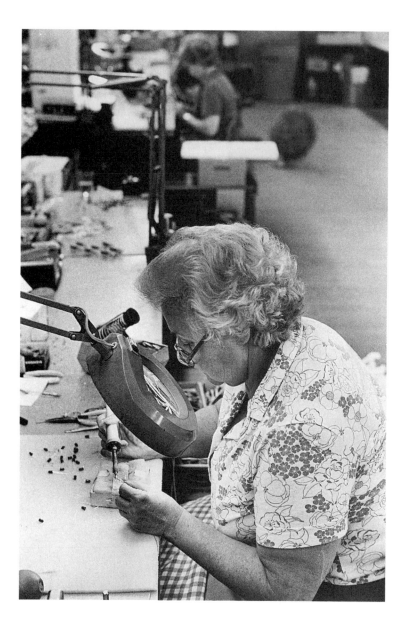

At different times in our lives we may need to change careers.

happening in your local area, in the United States, and in the world. You could learn how trade agreements between countries might affect jobs. You could learn which companies in your area are growing. You could learn how technology will change the way we get and use information. If you have such knowledge, you can better prepare for opportunities in the job market.

2. Take classes at a community college, four-year college, or university. Universities are often expensive, but most teachers will let you **audit** classes for free. You don't get credit when you audit classes, but it's a good way to stay current with changes in your chosen field. Also look specifically for adult learning programs. Such programs tailor their classes to the learning and lifestyle needs of working adults.

3. Join professional associations in your job field. Attend meetings to learn what others are doing that is new and interesting. Sometimes these professional associations have national conferences. People come from all over the country to share ideas and information. For example, teachers often go to conventions where they learn about the latest teaching practices. People in the computer industry, in manufacturing, and in other industries do so as well.

4. If you have outside interests or hobbies, keep them up. Take those drum lessons or yoga classes. Play touch football on the weekends. As you grow older and your human needs change, your outside interests may turn into a second career. For example, Martha had a long and happy career in nursing. Her outside interest was **genealogy.** She traced her own family history back more than 300 years. After 20 years, Martha left nursing to start her own business helping others trace their family trees.

5. Get out and be active in your community. Volunteer. You'll learn more about people and what's happening in the world than you ever thought you could. You will also feel great about giving something to a cause you believe in. If you find something you really love doing, it may become a second career.

One way to continue learning is to attend professional conferences.

Can you come up with another idea for lifelong learning?

There are really thousands of other ways to continue your lifelong learning. Engaging in these activities will help you prepare for the future, whatever it may bring.

Revising Your Career Plan

Is it possible to have one career plan all your life? A career plan that never needs to be revised?

Yes, it is possible. However, it is highly unlikely. Several times in this book, you've read that the average person changes jobs seven times in his or her lifetime. Many people do it more often. Each time you change jobs, it is a good idea to work through some or all of the career planning process. The level or depth at which you complete each step depends on your situation.

For example, suppose your company lays you off. You do a little reading about career trends. You learn that your career field still has many opportunities. The company you worked for was just poorly run. You assess yourself. You decide that the work you do is still rewarding to you. You decide to seek another position doing similar work. You research companies, write your résumés, and go to interviews. Finally you get hired. You work to be successful.

Now suppose you turn 40 and feel a great dissatisfaction. You've been doing the same job for 20 years. Things that once interested you no longer do. You begin back at Step 1 of the career-planning process. You feel like you're 16 again, making your first career plan.

A Quick Review of the Career-Planning Process

Step 1. Take a look at the big picture of career trends and the job market.

Step 2. Assess yourself and your lifestyle choices.

Step 3. Explore careers.

Step 4. Build a foundation for your career.

Step 5. Get hired.

Step 6. Be successful in your career.

Step 7. Continue planning.

Careers Practice

Answer these questions on a separate sheet of paper.

1. To prepare for changes in the world and changes in you, what kind of learning should you engage in?

2. Give one example of how to engage in lifelong learning.

3. How might pursuing an outside interest or a hobby help you in the future?

A Final Word About You

As you go off into the world of work, remember three things:

1. You are an important person.

2. You have something worthwhile to contribute to the world.

3. You have strengths that you can turn into successes.

It is up to you to make things happen. Use the processes in this book and all the resources around you. Learn from your experiences, good and bad. Good luck!

Chapter Review

Chapter Summary

- Many things can cause us to revise our career plans. Some of these are factors that affect the job market: technology, world events, and the changing population. Others are personal choices, unplanned events, and human needs.

- Some of the personal choices that could affect careers have to do with marriage and children. Unplanned events such as sickness, accidents, or divorce can also affect careers. In the event of any of these, we should reassess our career plans.

- Changing human needs can also affect our career plans. Dr. Abraham Maslow said there are five basic human needs: survival, security and safety, a sense of belonging, esteem, and self-actualization. With each need, we may seek different things from our professional or personal lives.

- One way to be prepared for the changes in the world and in ourselves is to engage in lifelong learning. There are many ways to continue learning. We can read and pay attention to the news. We can take adult education classes. We can pursue hobbies. We can join professional associations. We can also volunteer our time and be involved in our communities.

- The average person will change jobs seven times in his or her lifetime. At each of these changes, you can refer back to the career-planning process in this book. Complete all or some of the steps as necessary.

Chapter Quiz

Answer these questions on a separate sheet of paper.

A. Thinking About Careers

1. Technology, world events, and the changing population can cause us to revise our career plans. What three other factors can do this?

2. How could marriage cause a person to revise his or her career plan?

3. How could having children cause a person to revise his or her career plan?

4. Name two unplanned events that could cause a need for a career change.

5. Who was Dr. Abraham Maslow?

6. In Maslow's hierarchy, what is the first human need?

7. What is at the top of Maslow's hierarchy?

8. What is one thing we can do to prepare for the many changes in the world and in our lives?

9. To what are adult education classes tailored?

10. What is another way to continue lifelong learning?

B. Putting What You Learned to Work

Now that you're a career expert, write a short essay about the importance of planning a career. Include three of the most useful things that you learned from this book.

C. Work Out

Imagine yourself in 40 years. What kinds of things have you done? What experiences have you had? How did your career change over time? How did you continue to learn throughout your life? Write at least a page describing these things.

Unit Eight Review

Answer these questions on a separate sheet of paper.

1. What are job reviews?

2. What is a performance standard?

3. What two qualities make for a good performance standard?

4. List three things in the work environment that could hurt worker performance.

5. What is a career path?

6. What are two personal choices that could affect your career?

7. What are two unplanned events that could affect your career?

8. According to Maslow's hierarchy, what is the first need we must satisfy?

9. When we need esteem, what are we looking for?

10. What are seven steps in the career-planning process?

Appendix

Glossary

Index

Glossary

abbreviation   a shortened form of a word

accomplishment   a successfully completed task; an achievement

accounts receivable clerk   a person who keeps records of incoming money

acquaintance   a person known slightly, not someone who is a good friend or a relative

action verbs   words that show action, such as "run," "plan," or "direct"

activist   a person who works for change, usually for a social or political cause

agency shop   a business in which employees are not required to join a union but must pay union dues

alimony   any regular payment of money due to a separated or divorced person from his or her spouse

analyze   to examine closely

animal assistant   a person who assists veterinarians (animal doctors) in caring for animals

annual report   a book published yearly that describes an organization and its accomplishments

application   a form that a worker fills out when applying for a job

appoint   to choose a person for a particular job or task

appointment   an arrangement to meet at a certain time and place

apprenticeship   an on-the-job training program in which a skilled worker teaches someone a trade or craft

aptitude   a natural ability to learn or do something well

assess   to judge or set a value on

attainable   able to be gained or achieved

attendant   a person who serves or helps another

attitude   a mental outlook

audit   in education, to listen to or attend a class without being officially enrolled

authority   the power or right to give orders and make others obey

auto body worker   a person who repairs car and truck bodies

auto mechanic   a person who repairs the mechanical parts of cars and trucks

automotive technician   a person who builds, maintains, and repairs cars

baby boom   a sudden increase in the birth rate

billing clerk   a person who records and sends out bills

bonus something given in addition to what is usual or expected

bookkeeper a person who keeps records on business expenses and income

broadcast technician a person who installs, runs, and repairs equipment used by TV and radio stations

budget a plan of how to balance income and spending

bureaucracy an organization that has many levels and that has strict ways of doing things

business cycles alternating periods of growing and shrinking economic activity

candidate a person seeking a position

capital any money or equipment invested in running a business

career a chosen occupation

career counselor a trained professional who helps people with their career searches

career ladder a series of jobs that lead to greater responsibility and usually more money

career path a map or outline of how a worker could move or advance in a company

career plan an outline of what a person wants to achieve; it includes details of how the person wants to

achieve the goal; it also includes a time schedule

civil service the system that hires workers for government jobs

clerical relating to clerks or office workers

clerical supervisor a person who trains and oversees clerks

comedian a person who tells jokes and funny stories in front of an audience

commission a fee paid to a sales worker for selling goods or services, usually a percentage of the sale price

communication the transfer of information from one person or group to another

competition an attempt to get something that others want; a contest

computer service technician a person who installs, maintains, and repairs computers

cons the reasons *against* doing something

conservation the preservation of natural resources and environments

construction trades careers that involve the building of structures such as houses, highways, and bridges

consumer a person who buys goods or services

contract a verbal or written agreement made between two or more people or groups of people

contractor a person who manages building projects; the contractor usually hires workers as they are needed to complete the projects

cosmetology the study of make-up, hair styling, and other beauty techniques

costume designer a worker who designs and sews clothing for performers in plays and movies

counselor one who listens and offers ideas

cover letter a short letter to an employer that is included with a job application or résumé

craft guild an early organization of trade workers that was like a trade union

customer service representative a worker who provides information and solves problems for customers

cyclical unemployment a situation that occurs when people are out of work because of a downturn in the business cycle

data information

delay to put off

demographics facts or characteristics about a population

dental assistant a person who assists dentists with patient care

dental hygienist a person who cleans and takes x-rays of the teeth

direct sale the sale of goods or services directly to a consumer, not through a store

director a worker who coaches actors in a play or a movie

directory a published resource that lists information for a certain area or subject

disability the condition of not being able to do something

discipline training that develops character and self control

discrimination unfair treatment because of race, color, religion, or sex

diverse having many different characteristics, varied

diving technician a person who works on underwater projects

drafting technician a person who helps draw the plans for such things as buildings and machines

ecology the study of how all living things relate to one another and their world

elect to choose by voting

electrician a person who sets up or fixes electrical equipment

employee handbook a book or booklet that gives workers important information about the company that employs them

entitle to allow or give right to

entrepreneur a person who organizes and runs a business

environment all the things that surround and affect a person

ethics a system of rules or principles of behavior

evaluation a judgment of performance, such as a job review

exceed to go beyond what is expected

executive a person who helps run a business

facsimile machine a machine that sends written documents over the phone lines; also called a *fax machine*

feedback response from another person about how one has performed

file clerk a person who organizes paperwork and puts it into files

fire safety technician a person who inspects buildings for fire safety

flexible easily changed; bending easily

forestry technician a worker who assists in managing forests

franchise an arrangement between an entrepreneur and a business chain. The entrepreneur pays to use the chain's name and to sell its products or services.

fringe benefits any benefits given to workers other than wages, such as vacation pay, sick leave, health insurance, pensions, and so forth

genealogy the study of a family history or family tree

goods things which can be seen, touched, bought, and sold

gratification a sense of satisfaction or pleasure

hazardous waste harmful chemicals or other substances that threaten life

health technician a health worker who assists a health professional

heating and air conditioning technician a person who builds, maintains, and repairs heating and air conditioning equipment

hierarchy a ranking of things according to importance

home health care worker a person who cares for a sick or disabled person in the home

homemaker a person who manages a household

human resources department a department that screens job applicants and administers employee records and benefits; called the *personnel department* in some companies

income the money a person receives, usually for working or for providing a service

independent not influenced or controlled by others

informational interview a question-and-answer session between a person who is exploring a career and a person who has that career

interests things a person is curious about or likes to do

Internal Revenue Service (IRS) the bureau of the U.S. Treasury Department charged with enforcing the tax laws passed by Congress

internship an on-the-job learning and training program

investor a person who loans money to a business with the hope of making a profit

job review an evaluation of an employee by an employer

job sharing a situation in which two people share the responsibilities of a single job

journeyman a skilled worker who has mastered a trade

language arts writing, reading, speaking, and other communication skills

lateral transfer a sideways move within a company to a different department or to a different position

at the same level of salary and responsibility

leisure free time used for rest or recreation

licensed practical nurse (LPN) a nurse who has completed a training program in patient care

local government the level of government that manages counties, cities, and towns

machine trades careers that involve building, installing, running, and repairing machines

machinist a person who cuts, drills, and grinds metal into particular shapes and sizes

manufacture the making of goods with machines, usually in a factory

mechanic a person who makes, repairs, or uses machines

mechanical technician a person who installs, maintains, and repairs machines in plants or factories

memorandum a short written notice (*memo* for short)

mental health worker a person who treats people suffering from mental or emotional problems

mentor an experienced person who helps and advises an inexperienced person

military personnel the people who serve in a country's armed forces

minimum wage   the lowest hourly amount of money that a business can legally pay its workers

minority   a member of a group that makes up less than 50 percent of the population

mission   purpose

motivated   inspired to do something

national origin   the country where a person was born

natural resources   resources that are not made by humans, such as air, water, soil, and animals

negative   hopeless or pessimistic

negotiate   to bargain

net income   money earned minus the amount withheld

network   a system of connected lines that transmits information

objective   a step toward meeting a goal

Occupational Safety and Health Administration (OSHA)   the federal agency that is charged with inspecting businesses and enforcing safety laws

orderly   a hospital aid who helps care for patients

paralegals   people who assist lawyers

parent   a person who has the long-term responsibility of raising a child

park technician   a worker who assists in running a park

payroll clerk   a person who makes sure that paychecks are correct and that they're delivered on time

peer mentor   a person who has the same job responsibilities as another, but who is more experienced and can offer advice about the job

pension   a regular payment to a retired person by a former employer

performing arts   activities done in front of an audience, such as acting or playing music

persistence   continuing on a course of action even when difficulties arise

personality traits   the ways a person behaves; characteristics

persuade   to make someone willing to do or believe something

pharmacy assistant   a person who helps fill prescriptions

photojournalist   a person who takes photographs for newspapers and magazines

plastics technician   a person who helps develop and test plastic materials

policy   a general rule or philosophy about how things should be done

pollution control technician   a worker who tests water, soil, and air for harmful substances

positive   hopeful or optimistic

poverty line   the minimum yearly income that a family must have in order to meet its basic needs

prioritize   to rank in order of importance

probation   a trial period

procedure   a step-by-step outline of how a task is to be performed

production   the act of making something

professional association   an organization whose members all have the same occupation. Members of professional associations usually meet regularly to share information.

professional athlete   a worker who is paid to perform sports in front of an audience

profit   the money made by a business after all its costs have been paid

promotion   a change to a higher position or level

proofread   to carefully read a written piece and mark any corrections needed

pros   the reasons *for* doing something

prospect   a future possibility or chance

protégé   a person who is guided or helped by a more experienced person

public relations department   a department that is responsible for giving out information about an organization

quarterly   every four months

real estate   property

receptionist   a person who receives customers or guests in an office or hotel

recession   a period when the production of goods and services decreases for six months or more

recommendation   a written or spoken statement that someone or something is worthwhile or valuable

recreation aid   a worker who helps organize sports, crafts, games, and other enjoyable activities

recruiter   a person who gets others to join an organization such as a branch of the armed forces

recycle   to make something able to be used again; to use again

referee   a worker who sees that rules are followed by the players during a sporting event such as a football or basketball game

refuse collector   a worker who collects solid waste (garbage) and takes it to a landfill or recycling center

registered nurse (RN)   a nurse who has completed a two- or four-year program in patient care

rejection   a refusal; a turndown

research   careful study

resource   something that is available that we need or can use

résumé   a written statement of a worker's experience, education, and personal information

retail   having to do with selling directly to the public

retain   to keep or hold onto

retire   to leave a job or career, usually because of age

right-to-work laws   state laws that give people the right to work without having to belong to unions

robotics technician   a person who installs, maintains, and repairs robots

role model   a person who is admired, respected, and imitated by others

scout   a worker who looks for talented players and recommends that they be hired by another team

secretary   a person who answers phones, types letters, and performs other duties in an office

security   a feeling of safety; freedom from danger

self-actualization   a state of development that is reached when a person achieves his or her goals

self-esteem   self-respect

services   work performed for others, such as teaching or selling

set designer   a worker who designs and builds sets for movies and plays

sexual harassment   any unwelcome sexual advances or conduct

shipping and receiving clerk   a person in a stock room or warehouse who is involved with receiving incoming goods and shipping outgoing goods

skill   an ability to do something well

social security number   a number issued by the federal government for tax purposes

standards   set guidelines

stock clerk   a persons who shelves and packages goods in a stock room or warehouse

strategy   a plan

structural unemployment   unemployment that occurs when workers do not have the education or skills to fill available jobs

tax return   a worker's report to the government of how much the worker has earned, paid in taxes, and either owes in taxes or is due in a tax refund

technology   the use of science to create new or better products or methods of production

telemarketing   the selling of products and services over the telephone

temporary agency an agency that finds temporary jobs for workers

temporary lasting for a short time

theory an explanation of or ideas about a subject

ticket agent a person who provides facts about travel schedules, makes customer reservations, and sells tickets

trade magazine a magazine that contains articles and information about a particular industry

trade union an organized group of trade workers that attempts to get or maintain fair wages and working conditions for its members

transferable easily moved or exchanged from one place to another

trend general direction or tendency

tutoring one-to-one teaching

umpire a worker who sees that the rules are followed by players during a baseball game

unemployment rate the percentage of people in the labor force who are looking for work but have not found jobs

union shop a business in which all non-management employees must be union members

values the principles that a person holds to be important; standards or beliefs

veterinarian an animal doctor

visual arts activities such as painting, drawing, sculpting, and photography

visualize to form a mental picture of; to imagine

vocational school a school that trains people to do specific jobs or trades

W-2 form a yearly wage and tax statement sent by a business to an employee

W-4 form a statement that determines the amount of taxes withheld from an employee's paycheck

waste management the industry that cleans waste from the environment and safely stores it

waste water treatment operator a worker who cleans and treats water from sewers and businesses

wildlife technician a worker who assists in tracking and caring for animals in a natural setting

withhold to keep or hold back

word processor a person who enters letters and other written documents into a computer

Index